AF422586

Just Twelve More Poems
and other works

LitGarden Writers

Just Twelve More Poems
and other works

LitGarden Writers

Edited by George Grace and Kate Willoughby

Buffalo, New York

Copyright 2019 by LitGarden Writers
All Rights Reserved
Printed in the United States of America

ISBN 979-8-218-13974-2

Rights to all materials revert to the author or artist upon publication in this anthology. Reprinting of all materials is allowed only by permission of the author, artist, or the editors of LitGarden Writers, except for the use of brief quotations in a book review or scholarly journal. Some of these works may have been published elsewhere in a different form.

Copies of this publication may be purchased online, at book signing events, or by contacting George Grace at:

LitGarden Writers
ggraceart@gmail.com

Front cover art by George Grace, *LitGarden*

Back cover by Kate Willoughby, photo, *Reinstein Woods*

Layout/Design by Kate Willoughby

Edited by George Grace and Kate Willoughby

*"Vines need a trellis to lift up their arms,
grapes need a look at the sun…"*

- Victoria Hunter

Foreword

The LitGarden Writers group came together in 2008, when George Grace was remodeling Michael Delaney's house and mentioned that he would like to start another creative writing group. Michael expressed his own interest in writing, and so the construction of our workshop began. The first gathering of writers included Donna Grace, Manny Fried, Michael Delaney, Gary Earl Ross, Janna Willoughby, Sara Reis, and, of course, George Grace.

Altogether, over forty members have joined and contributed to the group during its first decade, each with their own individual stories and perspectives to share. This anthology is not an exhaustive catalog of all our collective work, but instead, it represents a faithful snapshot of the offerings of our current poets, diverse in disciplines and genres, and in our ages, backgrounds, and identities. We are students, teachers, artists, activists, travelers, judges, musicians, historians, and mathematicians. We are unified not by sameness of style, but by our substance and practice of providing support and inspiration to each other.

But we'll stop here before we bore you with our bio…
…or spend three minutes introducing a haiku.
If you would remain seated, we'd like to share
Just Twelve More Poems…

List of Art Works and Photographs

George Grace

George Grace is the author of three books of poetry—American Stonehenge; Night Wanes, Dawn; and Steeling America, a Poetic Memoir of Lackawanna's Steel Plant. His poetry has been published in Earth's Daughters, Pure Light Magazine, and many times in the Buffalo News' Poetry Page. He has also written seven plays, the most recent of which is under development, Gertrude Stein Reconstructed. He is the founder of Buffalo's second-longest running reading series, the Circleformance Lit./Music Series, and co-founder of the LitGarden writers group.

He has taught for Writers-in-Education, at Collins and Attica Correctional facilities, and has guest lectured on writing at Villa Maria College and Buffalo State. He is also a visual artist, past president of the Buffalo Society of Artists, and a former tournament chess player.

Peru

1.

The memory is a tricky thing,
often tangling its feet with imagination.
Mine tricks me into thinking I am still the volleyball player
I was at twenty-five when my young legs

could push me a meter or so toward the heavens
and my knees had the juice to cushion my fall back to earth,
when in fact none of these things work like they used to.

Yet the memory refuses to surrender to the evidence;
and so in my dreams I continue to waft
head above the tape of a volleyball net,
or at least imagine it is still possible to do.

That I have been to Peru is a shameless lie, but often
when I really do for the first time come upon such places,
I feel an odd familiarity
as if my memory works in reverse, as if
this is what Peru will look like
from the last time I was here.

Give me a map and sight unseen, sounds unheard,
I will know the topography, the people,
the best restaurants, the narrow streets to avoid.
I can't explain why this works for me.
I'm not claiming to be a psychic.

I have always found comfort in knowing where I am.
And why not? The world, so strange,
is breadth and width nonetheless my home.
It has always been vital I know the place of every doorknob
    and light switch.

2.

I met her in this "Peru."
The pigeons in the square were pecking near our feet
when her words killed me amidst Lima's teeming masses,

to a person indifferent to the murder
under the afternoon sun.

I walk the earth nonetheless, neither zombie nor ghost
none the worse for wear,
at least on the surface.

We lived a long life together apart.
Anguished by her crime, terrified of commitment
she remains hermetic.

Apparently I didn't know her as well as I knew Peru,
and I don't love Peruvian food as much as I remembered
though the people were, but for one exception

pleasant, like the groves of tropical fruits
and gardens I have seen only in photos.

3.

I awoke this morning with the fictional memory of Peru
stuck in my head. I wasn't sure why I left,
or what I left it for. Other lands, other loves?

Seeking memories to embrace at the expense
of living in real moments?
Did I need a reason to leave?

Perhaps none of this. This morning

I awakened in the city of my birth
having never strayed too far,
too long, from my home.

Pity.

Pity?
The painting I have just done
is of a place a short walk away.
It was from this painting that I learned
I didn't need Peru, fictional or real,
not its mountains, nor its lakes and rivers

and its people

though a pleasant lot

have clones worldwide.

Somewhere in Kentucky

I wonder if the people who own and work
the length and width of this land know that,
just beyond this forest's embrace,
amidst the banal bales of hay dotting
the dark and matted farm fields here,
the forlorn beacon lighting the garage roof there,
the promise of art lives,
now,
ten minutes after sunset,
a fleeting splendor in the ordinary,
imploring itinerant eyes to make it so.
I drove a thousand miles for a month's work,

and with home six hundred away,
my tired heart yearned to have you beside me,
in this zip code with more numbers than families,
mid-Kentucky, mid-winter,
the twilight cradling just enough color
to remind us of the road, the people, the day
we left behind.

When I stop to take photos
of places like these and you say,
yes, that's a lovely scene, you should paint it,
you are my antidote to solitude.
Tomorrow, at dawn, I will likely leave
some paneled motel room
twenty dark and tortuous miles
north of this frozen moment,
head out into the fog-shrouded valleys
awash in the promise of spring's light,

blessed that I didn't miss this journey,
even if diminished for you not being here to tell me,
yes, it happened, and it was ours.

Running on Fumes

Last time through this leg of US 219,
western third of Pennsylvania,
bearing north, August 1977,
an all-night drive up from Virginia Beach,
Sunday night/Monday morning,
a broke and broken man
who just wanted to get home to Buffalo
to heal wounds from a love, lights out and locked

like the gas stations and coffee shops
anchoring the dozens of towns, obsolete from birth.

Fifteen cents on my dash,
a chunk of my tire tread missing,
gas gauge at quarter-tank and diving,
nerves frayed by speed limits and stop lights
that have no meaning, not here, not now.
Which disaster strands me, moot.
Caring merely wastes energy.
I'll either make it home or I won't, I thought.

Whatever.
Serpentine road through hills.
Fog and forest splaying the light of
oncoming headlamps
like wagon wheel spokes,
every sluicing shadow suggesting a collision
with a deer, dog, raccoon,
any soft and innocent target.
I'd rather not kill anything, ever,
especially not tonight, please.
I have no reserve.

I suppose it's progress
that I don't live like that anymore,
so close to the edge,
crossing the city line, five miles to go,
running on fumes.

Sunday Night Rides Home from Cowlesville

seemed to take twice as long as long as the drive out
by the dozen clusters of buildings

too sparse to bother naming,
by the forgotten shards and droppings
of an aspiring young empire

by the closed gas stations/convenience stores
shoebox Lutheran and Baptist churches
distant farmhouses with auto-wreck graveyards
nestled between gravel driveways
and postage stamp cornfields.

I wore home the tired legs of whole days spent hiking
the wooded hills and ravines
around my best friend's town

keeping dad awake through his beer-benders
reminding him to stay in his lane
coaching him to follow the curves of the road
thinking, as often as not,

that my parents *must* have kidnapped me,
dooming me to a life of anonymity in the city,
thinking

that if I wasn't so young, so small,
they would never have pulled it off.

A half century later, when I relive
the long Sunday night rides home
down streetlamp-mottled two-laners,
past the matured and decaying outposts of America,
I prefer the upside of those bittersweet memories:

The tables of competing macaroni salad recipes.
The smell of grilled barbecue spearing my nostrils.
Glutting myself on watermelon.
Skidding through the mud to home plate
in pickup softball games

during the summers of a childhood
that lied to me when it promised
that winter was an eternity away.

Why I Heart My Blue State

Up at four AM, just couldn't sleep any more

trying to imagine the   mindset
of the Texas state lawmaker
who doubtless kipped up in bed   in a cold sweat
with an inspiration for a law
of such startling novelty   who

when he later headed to the state capitol
passing on his way thousands
of drought-stricken cattle-cadavers
to pitch this idea   found sufficient
if not enthusiastic

support   among his colleagues
to limit the acquisition   and ownership
of vibrating   tickling   chirping   gyrating
ersatz   male organs

to five.

Was there a debate over this?

>   *Let's limit people to seven dildos*
>   *and prohibit using them   with illicit drugs.*

No   no more than three   with background checks
with an additional penalty for using them
in the commission of a crime.

>   *Four, so long as they vibrate   not tickle.*
>   *Batteries must be recycled.*

Okay, let's go with five,
we ban importing Mexican dildos
and balance the budget.
>   *And cut taxes to our job-creators.*

Poetic revelation:
those suffering the existential pluses and minuses
of being Texans
can own hundreds of firearms   of every mm.
and caliber   they can afford

but god help the Texan who tries to buy that sixth dildo
offering without proof statements such as
I know I have five
but this one's for my mother's 83rd birthday
(she wore out the other four, you see).

I guess that the Texan mindset prefers
the type of penetration
that is lethal,

and executed from a safe distance.

Protocol

At Harper's Ferry, in the church at the top of the hill
perhaps Church of God-the-Micromanager
another tourist with no real stake but what
    to his thinking
amounted to his defense
     of God's ongoing and abiding concern
          for clothing dos and don'ts
went *psst!*
     pointed to his head & moved his hand
         to his waist.

I didn't get it. Was he soliciting money? Oral sex?
You're in a church, he said.
We remove our hats.

Having spent so little time since the age of consent
in Houses of God
    it just never occurred to me
         surprised me   annoyed me   struck me as
    idiotic
that on the order of spiritual contemplations and concerns
    Cardinal sins   religious crimes and misdemeanors
self-appointed arbiters of correctness
    amateur interpreters of God's mind   trailer-park Popes
for reasons that mystify me   have deemed
hat-removal   a measure of respect;
that their all-knowing   deity (not mine)
        might take offense   at my covering
for vanity   or warmth
      my thinning hair.

Fighting an urge which might lead to an insurrection
     reminiscent of John Brown's quest to end slavery,
         I said,
Oh.
    I'll leave instead.
Places like this/people like you give me hives anyway.

The Irony of Perfect Health

Never sick a day in his life,
she said of her father
and then it occurred to me
as I downed two cold & flu soft-gels
and chased them
with a glass of water,

this sounds like a joke in search of a punch line,
something like,

and then he died suddenly at forty-two from...

And this is where, you see, we get creative
because this whole sick idea of someone
being so blessed
cannot possibly inspire *imitation,* I thought,
blowing my nose--

since by age seven I'd already had been disqualified
by measles, mumps, & chicken pox,
numerous colds, earaches, and strep throat--

nor *admiration* (because what if the subject
was a Nazi, or a boss whose mission
was to make miserable
every hour of his employees' working lives?)
--in other words, is this a morality tale
with an amoral character as the subject?

And so by giving me a statement
bearing a divining rod in search of an ironic finish,
I mused,
adjusting my heating pad & pulling up my comforter,
unless the story continues

but he was ever on the verge of a nervous breakdown
expecting the other shoe to drop,

I can't imagine him having any other mission
than to devote the entire span of his long & healthy life
cooking chicken noodle soup
for the whole sneezing,
hacking, miserable
rest of mankind.

For the Man in the Third Row, Second Seat
from the Left at My Poetry Reading

I'm sorry,
after seeing your glazed eyes
half open mouth and blue nostrils,
for thinking you a dullard.

Perhaps my ten-minute poet's bio was a little
    excessive.
I didn't have to list *every* publication credit
including three want ads I wrote for the *Pennysaver,*

could have omitted details about my love of everything
from butterflies and oatmeal
to origami and stamp-collecting,

didn't need to name every pet I ever owned
and the three girls who gave me Valentine's Day cards
back in first grade.
For this, I'm sorry.

I need to apologize, too,
for the two-minute long introductions to my haikus.
For reading the poems I scribbled on the bus ride over.

For editing while reading them aloud.
And my ongoing self-critiques—
this line sucks and *I need a better verb here*—
were a little over the top.

I also want to apologize for announcing
I will finish by reading just twelve more poems.
In retrospect, that was a little selfish,
with six poets waiting to read after me.
Had I heard that, I might have had a cerebral hemorrhage.
Right there. On the spot.

But I was so absorbed with the thrill of reading
to a live audience
that I never considered the possibility that you,
the man in the third row, second seat from the left,
who never once smiled, nodded, or clapped

might be *dead.*

That said, I wonder if you were still alive

when I read my six-part poem
about grandma's gnarled hands.
It has a line that Carl Dennis once commented on,
which is saying something
because he won a Pulitzer for poetry
I sure hope you didn't die without hearing it.

Contemplations, Falling Twenty-Five Feet
Off a Ladder

Oh. The downspout
wasn't screwed into the
gutter.
That was really stupid,
 relying on it to steady
myself.
Yep, this is *not* a drill.
I'm going down.

I should let go of it.
I'll need both hands
to get me out of this
mess.
Ladder's gone.
Can't grab that.
Shit, one tiny mistake.
Does it have to be fatal?
Maybe not.

Relax, let it happen.
You can't stop it anyway.
If I twist around like a cat
and if push hard enough
off this window sill
I'll hit that garage roof
and it'll break my fall.

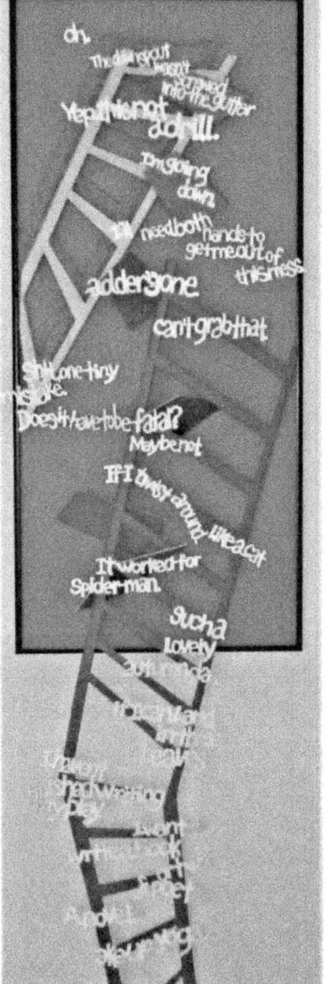

It worked for Spider-man.
Such a lovely autumn day.
The quality of light dancing across the autumn leaves
is like an eye-symphony.

Okay, the pushing-off part
didn't work as well as I'd hoped,
but if I can land in those leaves,
maybe my upper torso will be spared injury.

I can't die yet. Not at thirty.
I don't want an obituary that reads:
    He was, well, a guy who,
    well, breathed and ate.
    He also had hair.
            And fingernails.

The homeowner is going to be very upset.
I thought I was destined for greater things,
none of which will happen if I'm dead.
I won't be able to make any more art,
learn the lead to *Stairway to Heaven,*
or quit smoking.

I'd like to get laid a few more times—
at least once more, one for the angels,
by someone who loves me. For a change.

If I live, I'll have to clean up the paint.

Can't have a bunch of friends at my funeral,
spewing banalities like:

    He looks better dead than alive.

    I think Ronald Reagan drove him to this,
    with that trickle-down bullshit.

I haven't finished writing my play,
I want to write a book or two of poetry.
A novel.   Take up yoga.

That window needs glazing.
The owner's probably losing a lot of heat out of it.

Glad I got to see the Grand Canyon this summer.

I wish I'd gotten my bachelor's degree.

I could go for some BBQed wings right about now.

Amazing I'm able to think so many things,
given the time I have to impact.

If I survive, I should write a poem about this.
    Nah, that's a dumb idea.

Kate Willoughby

Kate Willoughby is a writer, musician, and retired Buffalo teacher living in a poor man's Victorian on the West Side. Her poems and stories have appeared in the *Buffalo News, Nickel City Nights* and the speculative fiction anthologies, *A Flash of Dark, Volumes 2* and *3*. She has also adapted and written children's plays based on classic literature. Her current passions are swing dancing, pie baking, and working in community Grassroots Gardens.

"Save your fork, there's pie!"

Since Columbine

Every year since Columbine,
I've had to have that talk with my class,
my eight-year-old third grade students, my babies,
who sit every day in that sunny circle on the rug, to
    retell a folktale,
    sing "Big Beautiful Planet"*,
    bust a move,
    play the cello,
    act out a fable,
    share a sorrow,
    snicker at a knock-knock joke.
Today they sit, quietly (in itself unusual),
while I tell about the special safety drill we will have.
    Their eyes are moons in dark water.

I explain to them
how we don't leave even if the fire bell rings,
how we keep the door locked even if somebody bangs on it,
how we kneel on the floor and cover our necks,
how we don't giggle - or scream - even if we hear shots
(here, their child soul dies a little).
    I don't say how I, Miss, will stand by the door,
my sturdy metal chair ready -
to knock the AR-15 out of the shooter's hands,
should he smash through the door's frosted glass -
ready to do whatever I can to stop him, which includes
ramming my body into his to block whatever bullets
I can from hitting my class, my babies, before I die,
so they can have a chance to run.
    Then we close by singing "Stand By Me"*.
"Miss, Miss", calls out Franklin, "What if I fall down?"
"Who will stop to carry Franklin?" I ask.
Thirty hands go up.

                     * by Raffi, 1982
             * by King, Leiber, and Stoller, 1960

Lament

Cut my hair with scissors,
rip the hems from my dresses,
blind the mirrors and cover the clocks,
for an evil—a falsehood, a coward, has
knocked out the lamps, struck down the pens,
trampled the truth on the clean floor.

The cries of young girls in pain,
mothers' moans as babies sicken
hacking coughs and bent knees of miner men,
breaking hearts of lovers kept apart,
make alt-right music to their neo-dance.

Last night, I passed an old man sitting on some cardboard,
his back against the bus station wall,
Army jacket collar turned up,
who said to me
 " 'Scuse me, miss I ain't had nothin' to eat today."
I gave him two quarters I had in my pocket
and he spoke again.

"Cease to lament for that thou canst not help,
and study help for that which thou lament'st.
Time is the nurse and breeder of all good."*

*The Two Gentlemen of Verona, Act III, I,
-William Shakespeare

Resist

(for Rebecca Solnit)

I am a bag of anger
filled to the top with lumps of coal-black carbonized
burnt sugar, all the sweetness gone bitter.

I'm no true heir of the Puritans,
whose satisfaction seeps from joyless bile.
Lovers of despair, they preen in
mirrors of self-righteousness.

Nor am I the Buddhist— setting hope aside
on a cleaned-off table where nothing is lost,
everything changes, and karma's a bitch.

Forget the evangelicals, the papist martyrs' flagellation—
disasters, double-headed lambs, rains of blood,
are not portents of a taking-up.

Fear of hell, chance of heaven?
There's only hope for here and now,
for what I can do about it.

My lot stands with the dogged pragmatists
who get up in the morning, risk their hearts,
get wetted by tears, and dirty of hands.

Seeking fire, I dump my sack of
charcoal in the pit.
Anybody got a light?

In Defense of Shakespeare

"What, art thou mad? Art thou mad?
Is not the truth the truth?"
 - Falstaff, King Henry IV, Part I, Act II, iv, 224

William, I believe you wrote them all.
No Jack authority can dampen the
run and roar of your battle words
or chill the heat of passion, wail of despair,
spark of glee you conjure
by swearing falsely that one man could not know,
could not know alone what you did see, what you did know.

You studied, read, and wrote
in fearful times much like our own;
made men and women, paupers and kings your textbook,
learned treachery at your father's knee,
secrets of politics, vices of religion, seduction of war.
Thousands of cold nights, you wrote alone,
instructed by your own failed love and loss,
Your hands like hennaed houris, covered in ink,
The Chronicles of England your pillow and your altar,

Today as well we know the rot of lies.
A plague upon those pint-potted tallow brains
who take from good
just to see it done,
to make us less.
A Falstaff sits upon our throne, a pillow on his head,
proclaiming,
"Lord, Lord, how this world is given to lying!"*
                *King Henry IV, Act V, iv, 144

At Three in the Morning

three fire trucks scream down the
one way street the wrong way,
flash in front of our house.

I wake up sharp in bed
ready to gather my valuables: husband, phone, and cat.
But the sirens are not here for us.
No fire or calamity erupts at number seventy.
My husband sleeps on, oblivious, snoring.
In slippers and coat I shiver out to the porch.
Three EMTs run into our neighbor's house.

A Jeep roars up the narrow street,
throbbing sub-woofers rattling windows.
One girl, home from a late night party
stumbles out of the car
laughing with the bigmouth bray of the deeply inebriated.

Trucks jam the road and her driveway.
"What the fuck!?"
yells the driver out the window, laying on the horn.

Out here the moon faced all there was to see:
the trucks, the drunk girl, the flashing lights, and me.

What I Am
(for Marge Piercy)

At last night's cocktail party
a friend asked me what I wanted to be
"now that I am retired",

as if I am not anything right now.

I want to be a climbing rose, a cherry tree,
a violet in the forest, a lake in July,
the song and flash that is a running stream,
the look in a bride's eye,
the step and swing of a street dancer,
the smack of a bat at a fastball,
the clean smell of waxed floors in an old house,
I want to be the next kind word from a teacher, a mother,
a lover.

I am not the answer to someone's crisis,
a target for their puritan disappointment,
Marge Piercy's burned liver, burned on purpose.

One child gets a new job, another loses his.
Husband pulls away, friend has no time.

But I am the wind that made the arches,
I am the fawn curled up against the headstone,
safe in the tall grass.

Ode to Pie

Something perfect
comes to mind in a sharp flash—

smell of wood cut in our father's shop
leather of a baseball glove,
rain smell on hot sidewalks.
Motown's music in your feet,
Doo-lang doo-lang
he's so fine,
or
a piece of work you make
with your own worn, cool hands.
Like pie.

Summer pie of peaches,
autumn apple
winter berry,
springtime lemon,
crust crisp and dry,
salty and sweet tart of it,
burnt sugar dripping.

A garden rose in bloom,
a sonata played,
something made
to be consumed and remembered -
more perfect
in that it doesn't last.

Sacrament

The sun leans down in an amber bowl
behind the Allegany hills
as I walk barefoot,
a penitent in the fields,
mourning for faith I've lost.

Naked aluminum women
spread their arms
over the man-made lake.

Like the faithful,
their eyes are milk,
looking only straight ahead.

Even a bare-faced atheist like me
can come, seeking benediction.

I dip my foot
in their font of stillness,
my eyes looking wide and far,
blessing myself and moving on.

I Set a Bowl

I set a bowl of soup in front of you—
a white china bowl with a green border.
Cream of tomato soup with jalapeños.
I warned that it was very hot.
You said it really had a kick.

I stood there looking out the window.
A cardinal shot to the fence in scarlet cassock
and cap ecclesiastical, singing in our trumpet vine
his invitation to confession -
his juris church my garden.

I said my silent mea culpas,
my litany of things I had not said or
things I said and should not have— for these
and all other sins which I cannot now remember—
I am truly sorry.

For times that I was with you, but not fully with you,
for times I could have touched you
but made my hands too busy.
I took the best tomato, left you without a goodbye kiss,
made small talk for fear of saying something real.
For these, I seek absolution.

The bird inclined his head and began a clear kyrie:
Here is mercy, he sang, *and here, your penance,*
now reconciliation I give to you.

You came over and we watched him closely examine a
nearby twig
in benediction
and fly off out of sight.

In kissing me,
you let your soup grow cold.

Street Civics

I read it in the *News* this morning - fourteen students in Rhode Island are filing a class action suit against their state education department for failing to teach *civics.* Rhode Island has no civics requirement, and does not have any teacher training in civics. The students claim the state fails to teach them how to prepare to vote, to understand taxes, to be on a jury, how to be intelligent contributors in the political system of our country.

I barely had time to shake my head over this travesty when I heard the roar of my neighbor's leaf blower— cursed noise polluter— and smelled the gasoline fumes. I slapped down the paper, pushed aside my tea, donned hat, coat and work gloves, dug out my long handled rake and biodegradable leaf bags, and forged out to do battle for the common good.

By this time, the neighbor, Vern, went back inside, having chased all his leaves out into the middle of the street. They were now liberated to blow, with the next stiff breeze, back into his yard as well as into everyone else's. Or the leaves might remain in the road, where rain and innumerable car tires would flatten them into muck, where freezing, thawing, and rotting would create a brown sludge impervious to salt.

In our neighborhood, you see, there is no special vacuum sucker truck for leaf collection like they have in the more affluent suburbs. The city street cleaner truck comes by our little one-way street twice a year, managing somehow to leave the street even dirtier than it was before. So we rake up some leaves for mulch, and bag the rest, taking care of our own piles.

I sighed into the cold air, fragrant now with damp earth and mold, since the gas smell dissipated. A few leaves still clung onto branches, too stubborn to give in to autumn's mandate. I began to rake my own yard. Even though I mostly have evergreens - spruces, arborvitae, and junipers, the leaves from close neighbors make themselves at home on my lawn. I scooped up the colors and shapes of oak, maple, and Chinese elms, along with some chickadee-and-squirrel-eaten pine cones. Then I started on the debris in the street, shoveling it into the leaf bag.

Vern came back out, sat on his porch steps, just watching me.

"Ya don't have to do that, why don'tcha leave it there? It'll dry up sooner or later, and the wind'll just blow it away."

I didn't answer right away, hoping to prepare a thoughtful, peace-keeping, neighborly "aw shucks" kind of answer. I considered a diatribe on tidiness, or a lecture about consideration for one's neighbors. Maybe I'd work up some kind of righteous "get a mulching lawnmower then" suggestion. Or maybe I could just go off on his ass for making extra work for others. And so what if he thinks I'm a crazy bitch—maybe that will increase his respect for me.

Nah, I decided, and just kept raking, bagging, smiling, raking some more, showing him how it all worked.

Diner

(SET: A slightly run-down 1940's vintage city diner,
windows letting in the grey afternoon light of late
autumn.)

HARRY: (Walks in, sits down at long counter. He looks
around as if looking for someone, his grizzled jaw
works as he takes off his hat.)

ADELE: (Plunks down a coffee cup in front of him.)

HARRY: Got any good pie?

ADELE: Got pie.

HARRY: Is it any good?

ADELE: That's a matter for the judge. (Whisks away to
wait on other customers.)

HARRY: (To JUDGE TAYLOR, sitting at counter eating
pie) How's the pie?

JUDGE TAYLOR: Not bad.

HARRY: Good. (A little louder) I'll have the pie.

ADELE: You'll have it and like it. (Slams plate with pie
down in front of him.)

HARRY: You seemed to like it last night.

ADELE: I must have been drunk.

HARRY: Not too drunk. (Enter Eddie, a rheumy-eyed old
guy in a battered raincoat and hat, sits down next to
HARRY.)

EDDIE: Somebody call me?

HARRY: Yeah, Eddie. (To ADELE) Black coffee here.
(Takes out a cigarette, puts it in his mouth, goes to light

it, then realizes he can't smoke it, keeps it in his mouth. ADELE plunks cup of black coffee in front of EDDIE.)

EDDIE: (To HARRY) She get up on the wrong side of the bed?

ADELE: No, just the wrong bed.

EDDIE: Harry, she's mad at you, I can tell.

HARRY: How can you tell, Eddie?

EDDIE: 'Cause you got a sad look in your eye, Harry, I can always tell. What'd ya do? Musta been something.

ADELE: It was something. A man can't call and tell somebody they're all right. I'm watching the news, Eddie. Homicide detective arrests suspect in fatal shooting, shots fired, two officers wounded. They don't name names until next of kin…

HARRY: A man can't always take the time to call. I got a job to do. You know that, baby.

ADELE: He comes to my place last night all hollow-eyed and what am I supposed to do, boot him out? (She blows her nose in a tissue.)

HARRY: She got up to make me coffee, Eddie. She sure can cook.

EDDIE: You two are all right now, ain't ya? I can tell, Harry, you two are all right.

HARRY: Drink your coffee, Eddie.

END

Donna Grace

Currently working as a substitute teacher in the Buffalo Public Schools, Donna Grace co-hosts the LitGarden Writer's Group.

As a Common Council Aide for the West Side in the 1990s, Donna responded to thousands of constituent complaints of neighborhood prostitution solicitations by establishing a non-punitive, educational court referral program that resulted in a less than 1% recidivism rate. Her efforts earned the Erie County Health Department a commendation from the Federal CDC, and gave the Buffalo Police Department a national Community Policing Award.

After successfully organizing the Elmwood community to stop Carl Paladino's plans to expand Rite Aid, she ran for Common Council, losing in a six-way primary to the mayor's chosen candidate. Donna is an activist for universal health care, climate change, and women's racial and economic justice. She is inspired by the writings of Rebecca Solnit and Eve Ensler, and is a fan of Marc Maron's podcast, *WTF*.

Pilgrimage

My husband says
let's take a ride
in the old Bethlehem Steel plant
so I can take photographs.
We enter Three Gate at dusk
travel crumbling roads
through ruins of
once mighty industry.
Gravel pings
against the car doors
dignity crunches under our wheels.

In the shadow of tall moldering coke ovens
a squat electrical machine shop sits
grasping at brick and mortar
begging for time
its door, red-faced
bears all the shame
the porch light
a beacon calling out
for the next shift to begin.

You drive slower, reminiscing.
I watch the young version of you
close the door to the work shed
flick a cigarette into the empty lot outside my window
take that leap like a cat from a hot tin roof,
        from being crushed between rail cars, or burned
alive, or suffocated in a cloud of deadly gas.
I see Big Daddy tying a car hitch to a guardrail
as a practical joke
and Slippery driving one of his
twenty-five-dollar death traps.

Driving through the gate
you pull onto the main highway.
Gripped by generations of grief
I lean back and open the window
so the wind can send this sorrow
soaring and wafting like a blue silk scarf
instead of bearing down with all of its dead weight.
How could I have known a photo expedition
would turn into a pilgrimage to a graveyard
of labor long forgotten?

I can barely remember
the melancholy face of my father
who will soon be dead more years than he lived
standing alone, nearby,
through a thicket of leggy pokeweed
while his two brothers, who lived to grow old,
linger in the distance, hands in pockets,
steel toe boots kicking up memories
sharp, shiny splinters
of a disintegrated Irish family.

I no longer wonder why
I search for my father
through old photographs of steel mills,
for the arrangement of machinery,
feel the searing heat oozing sweat from every pore
in the open hearth that took forty years
to grind him down.

Somewhere between
blood-soaked shirts on the picket line
and last call at Curly's gin mill
he dreamed in aquamarine,
of golf games at sunrise,
swan dives at sunset

cradled in a hammock
on a palm tree beach
until his time would drift to a stop.

For George

We sit in the breakfast room
sipping coffee and dining on conversation
sharing thoughts and feelings about yesterday
when you worked outside in 88 degrees,
how good it felt to finish rebuilding the deck
so you could move on to the next phase,
inside, where the air is cool,
where the cats flirt with you to pick them up.

We laugh at memories of mishaps,
falling off ladders, broken tools, spilled paint.
I marvel at you, the man of a dozen talents
who devises perfect solutions
deemed impossible by even the
best-schooled engineers and architects.

We talk about the history book I'm reading
of America's soul in search of its better angels
Native genocide, slavery, Jim Crow,
scorched earth economics
trigger happy police
desperate people with nothing to lose.

This walk we take with words
traveling between us
are moments relived,
so we don't risk forgetting.
Voyages of discovery

through eyes ripened
since the balmy August evening we met
thirty-three years ago.

Set adrift from the life I once knew,
you walked in
like a sheriff with his posse of friendly faces
who soon gathered round
and swept me up in friendly, familiar conversation.

You grab the cat as he walks by.
He lets out a squeak.
You cradle him in your arms
plant dozens of kisses
on his tiny forehead
carry him into the kitchen
for his morning pill.
I hear the pill drop and roll on the floor.
'C'mon, let's go', you say,
cajoling him to stop fighting this losing battle
then declare victory over his puny gullet.

You head back to your cluttered office studio
to tap out words on the keyboard for your book project,
deepen a few shadows on a painting
half listen to the teevee
where voices emanate all the way from the black box
into my ears
three rooms away.

To Rosie

At a coffee house called *Undergrounds*
with a *Rest in Peace* garden patio
cream-ation station
and other pun and funnery
embracing its funerary past,
.

the last time I sat in this room
was with you
half a lifetime ago
where your big brother Jack lay in his casket
up the stairs and down the long hallway,
where a string of booths reside
in the coffin corner.

*Death by asphyxiation at his job
in the grain mills,* they said.

The men called him a *fine lad,*
a high compliment in those parts,
in those days.

Muscles bulged under his Sunday blues
white collar secured with a tie
like a chokehold.
Pale skin luminescent against
the white satin pillow,
coils of black curls,
and eyelashes thick as whisk brooms
that would have made his blue eyes sparkle.

I walked through those same doors
you and I walked through together,

when you sobbed and grabbed hold of my arm,
afraid to go in, afraid to go on, afraid to let go.

In that tight-knit enclave,
when somebody died, everybody came.

Though you tucked your grief inside,
your brows gathered like storm clouds.
Tears dripped from your eyes like a soft rain.
The crowd parted to make way for your sorrow
that made grown men cry.

I looked up at the old lantern chandeliers
still hanging like pendants by their chains.
No table lamps or torchéres
casting their ambient light of pink gauze
that draped over us
like a pall.

I imagine you and Jack
sitting by the window in this coffee shop,
in shorts, sandals, and sunbeams,
reminiscing over French press coffee.

Jack recalls the pink bike you got for Christmas.
You named her Rainbow,
after the iridescent streamers he made
from spools of holiday ribbons
that burst from the tips of your handlebars
so when you tore down the street
like a pint-sized hurricane,
they would fly out, horizontal, like your pigtails.

You recall his third-grade crush, Sheila.
Her lace-trimmed ankle socks with pink bows,
black patent leather Mary Janes,

long brown ringlets
tied with silk ribbons
that always matched her dresses
made him blind and lovesick.
He snuck out to visit her every single day
even when she had the measles
while your mother was at work.

You were glad he wasn't there
to see the angry look on your mother's face
when you told her that story, in the nursing home.
It was too much to hope for,
to share a laugh, a cry,
to ease each other's pain, if even a little.

What you really ever came for
was a glimpse of the mother
who left you so long ago.

Chestnut Ridge

Beware of geese in a bad mood,
bickering over nesting rights,
attacking intruders.
Even in this great expanse
of ponds and shorelines
pettiness and envy reside.

A young couple from India
asks if we know the way to the Eternal Flame.
Sort of, I say.
Two hours in, the man
checks the compass on his phone.
He asks if we are lost.
Yes, probably, I say. We laugh.

No one came prepared
as we slide down muddy slopes,
hop rocks over streams swift and swollen
by snowmelt and spring rains,
crawl under felled tree trunks,
cold feet soaked in ankle boots,
leaky Wellies, porous Duckies.

Groves of delicate hemlocks
adorn ravines and sway in the crisp breeze.

Retracing our steps,
we come to a familiar place
that we walked by hours ago.
and there it is, in blazing orange letters
Eternal Flame: Straight Ahead.
I watch my three companions
navigate the greasy incline.
I know my limitations.

I hike my way back, up up up the steep, slippery trail
breathing hard, grabbing hold of trees and roots,
finally reaching level ground.
I hear faint voices
and lag behind the small family with a dog
until they veer off on another trail.

Ambling alone now, breathing in the silence,
sunlight sparkles off puddles and droplets.
I don't feel the stillness until
a rush of wind brushes against the trees.
I don't smell the air until I step on Douglas fir needles
and catch their sweet citrus aroma.
A tiny field mouse scampers along a mossy log
A red-tailed hawk screeches and soars overhead.

Diego

The notes that drift through my window screens
are the requiem of a broken heart
as the beagle next door, twelve now,
disturbs the morning
with soulful cries for his dead brother.

We take long walks together,
paws and feet a festival of motion.
When he stops to pee on a fireplug,
I say softly, *Oh, Diego, you're such a cliché.*
Soothed by the sound of a human voice
he stops and looks back at me.
I kneel down and wrap him in my arms.

We mourn together

in private rooms
like we did before vanity's scorn
of faces contorted with despair
recalling a lifetime
of death and loss.

When did we begin to prefer our grief
cool and sterile and silent
kept buried under layers of sorrow,
celebrating life with music and stories,
no messy cries of agony,
no tears spilling over the brim?

Diego's cries awaken memories
of near and far and long ago
of all the lives I've moved through
of all the lives who've moved through mine.

The Day We Woke Up With Cancer

We padded around in our slippers
like we do on early brisk mornings
to the comforting sounds of radiators
hissing and knocking.
I wrap the terry robe close to my skin.

The cat disappears into the bowels of some deep closet
postponing his morning pill
after a night-long fast
before the hour-long wait to let the medicine settle in
a ritual to keep him healthy and alive
taking the slow road to the inevitable.

I will chase him down, later,
after I finish my coffee,
before the CT Scan, the blood work,
the x-rays, pacing around waiting rooms,
staring at books I can't concentrate on.

We savor dark roast, two cups each,
with a generous shot of half and half.
It may surprise you, on mornings like this,
you become like the cat, clinging to routine
you never paid attention to before.

We head out on icy roadways.
The sun peeks over the horizon,
paints the town in blues and pinks
crisp, pellucid, shimmering
silky mist suspended
the sun catches on blades of grass
glints on the caravan of frosty cars
prisms ricochet off beveled glass windows.

I pull up to the front door and stop
on the circular driveway.
We kiss. *I'll meet you in a few minutes*, I say,
as I watch you walk into the building
and disappear into the thicket of
hairless, bloated, ashen-faced patients
in surgical masks and wheelchairs.
The man behind me toots his horn.
I don't know how much time has passed.

Leaving

So much has been said about
spring that it's become cliché
to be sad when it's time
to rake the horse chestnut leaves
from their landing pads,

the ones who made it to the finish line
from summer's canopy
to piles of withered umber
that sheltered and nourished
soil, earthworms, microbes
and now willingly
surrender their remains
after a long winter
in the flower garden
under a snowy shroud.

When the Quiet Comes

That first spring morning
surrounded by silence
I took a walk
in search of a robin
clamoring in the trees
or a bluebird roosting in a nesting box.

I thought of the peregrine falcon
raising her chicks on the skyscraper ledge
the osprey gliding down to rest on a lamppost
in a supermarket parking lot,
the mated pair of red-tailed hawks

swooping and soaring above the forested cemetery.

I once lived in a house
surrounded by a picket fence
where I'd wake at sunrise
just to watch the cardinals and blue jays
perched on the wooden slats
glistening in swirls of mist.

I once saw a photo in a magazine,
of American crows with midnight blue mantles
and gunmetal coverts
mobbing a man whose face they still recognized,
and deemed dangerous
for killing a hatchling
long, long ago.

A novelist adopted a starling
she named Carmen
for a book she wrote about Mozart
and his pet starling he named Starling
whom he adopted after hearing him sing,
through the open doors of the pet shop,
the opening bars of
Piano Concerto No. 17
in G

An author wrote a book about the adventures of
a boy and his goldfinch,
only it wasn't about an actual bird
but a famous painting by Fabritius
of a goldfinch chained to its perch.

An artist created replicas of
vultures, hawks, eagles, and ospreys
with hooked beaks that command your attention

from their pedestals
with black eyes that stare out
from broad, white crowns.
You can almost hear
the flap of silver pinnate wings,
imagine husky legs pressing down
on deadly talons
ready for flight.

As I walk home,
I hear another songbird singing,
You don't know what you've got 'til it's gone,
in her maple syrup voice,
the one with long vanilla hair
whose lyrics make you cry.

Bootstraps

On a busy, snowy street downtown
on the way to the bus stop
in my hand-me-down coat,
frayed collar and too-short sleeves,
a stranger barged through my
territorial imperative
poked his finger into my sternum
and said, *Girly, you better pick yourself up
by your bootstraps!*
before vanishing into the bustle.
I inspected my zip-up rubber overshoes
trimmed with fake fur that my
mother bought at the Liberty Shoe Store.
I veered into a made-in-America department store,
found the shoe guy
and told him, *Show me your selection of bootstraps.*

He glowered and said,
We don't sell bootstraps, only boots with straps.
OK, I said.

The shoe guy emerged from the back room
teetering behind a stack of swaying shoeboxes
that got the better of him--
box lids flew, tissue paper soared,
and a cascade of boots scattered.
Mid-calf lace-ups in patriot white, or amber waves of grain;
riding boots in gold refine with horsehair tassels;
purple mountain hiking boots with straps on both sides
for easing lifting;
WWII jackboots in star spangled alabaster, or Dust Bowl
red;
and finally, platform stiletto-heeled
thigh-highs with a dizzying cavalcade of laces, straps, and
buckles,
in spacious skies blue, or fruited plain berry.

I grabbed hold of those bootstraps,
pulled myself up, and just hovered there.
What a thrill to imagine
what I can do now,
on my pedestal,
the world at my pilgrim feet.

Dana

In gray November
on a perfect day for making stew
or taking long walks through fall leaves
in the quiet urban graveyard
we listen and speak to each other
tangled in the weeds of conversation.

A woman screams.
A coyote dashes by
and disappears into the mist.

I yell hello.
It's Dana who appears over the rise.
We walk up to meet her, down again, and
across the lane.
She points to the young buck 30 yards away
eating one of the apples
she feeds the small herd
breaking all the rules.

We gaze at him,
he gazes back, dazed, it seems
until he lifts his front leg,
broken, dangling.
Dana says she is full of regrets now
for interrupting the natural order of things
postponing the inevitable.

I first met Dana along the familiar route
she travels down to take a run
and leave apples for the deer
she told me of finding Clare slumped against a tree
 in the bloody shirt where the rifle bullet
 pierced her broken heart.

Lynn Ciesielski

Lynn Ciesielski taught children and adults with disabilities for over twenty years. When she retired she got very involved in writing poetry which she has been doing ever since. She has been published in *Helix, Buffalo News, Iodine, Main Street Rag* and a good number of other journals and newspapers. Lynn has also written two books, the first a chapbook called *I Speak in Tongues* published by Michael Czarnecki of Foothills Press and the second a full length publication called *Two Legs Toward Liverpool* published my Main Street Rag. Lynn has hosted *Circleformance*, a monthly poetry and music series since 2013.

Cross Purposes

We are surrounded by tree sighs,
voices that call back, even when
I speak in gentle tones,
mine far louder than these still,
pre-Cambrian ferns, fossils buried
beneath regrowth forest two centuries old,
I am a youth, yet
to my tentative truths, a crone.

Treading deep, the forest wraps us
in swaddling clothes.
Through my husband's eyes,
this forest is a lobster trap.

After two hours of crossed trails
we agree that the human imprints
I'd sought to escape, a mowed meadow,
wheels on asphalt, fence posts,
could be the just the compass we needed.

Arms wide, we run toward or away from what
neither knows, then nearly out,
I blacken my fingers with berry blood,
thanking him with the greater share of the berries.
He distrusts even these harmless gifts of the forest.
Betrayed, not a partner in my covenant
with this place he finds so unforgiving.

Happiness
      after Robert Hass

On this day of my lost resolve
after five hours of drag races,
you combed my hair into fine lily filaments,
once again demonstrating
how you nurture
even my heart's unidentified yearnings.

Upon returning home
we sat on the porch glider
chatting with neighbors,
enjoyed the balmy evening air
that dipped low like a fishnet
after so many rays of piercing sunlight.

We swung back and forth
like our moods always do.

We ventured to the Parkside Candy Shoppe
where a scoop of ice cream
meant forays into romance
in the circular room with frescoes,
glass cases, and striped wallpaper.
We spooned our favorite flavors
from crystal goblets, reminding us
that our sweet love tastes
like nothing else in the world.

At Kodak Film Plant

I read a story about the Kodak film company,
shut down except plant thirty-six,
where workers, who make film for Hollywood,
spending forty years in pitch black,
emerge wearing thick dark glasses and white suits.

I share the story with my sister Marge,
union men and women working
forty years in these conditions,
four hundred eighty months of polar winter.

They can retire after thirty years, but few places
support these moles' adaptation to the dark,
their eyes now as photo-
sensitive as a museum painting
except caves, underground tunnels, mines.

I compare it to life in Alaska.

Your analogy is flawed, Marge said.
It's not always like that in Alaska.

But it is, I say, *for months on end.*

My sister Marge lives in a black and white world
and needs to bend to see the light.

Black Ice

Twelve years later cautions still pierce
my pedal foot like the shattered glass
embedded in my daughter's jawline.
My only memory is breakfast
at the Greek dive, gyro and eggs,
pancakes for her to start the Saturday
after Friday payday run for two cartons
of Newport from the Seneca res.

Then,

Can't drive, shouldn't drive, never drive again,
my sister says, *You'd be stupid*
and I don't waste my time on stupid people.

But hey, we're here for you, Mom says.
Try this class. It's for the brain-injured.
You'll fit right in.

And I feel smart enough but we play checkers
and learn to cook canned soup.
Across from me a man who can't remember

his name or how to use a spoon
stares past a woman who babbles
about her tenth birthday and her first puppy.
I never return but after a year
of gearing forward I skid back
into the teaching gig I thought I'd lost
where we all knew the kinship
of something severed, broken, not stupid.

No need to drive, just wake early, catch
the number twenty, transfer twice and

I'm still left with an hour to spare.
The kids and I heal together while the snow
comes, numbing the pain until April
melts my brain to mud again,
this time from the inside and detritus
like shit makes it too ugly to overlook.

The doctor says, *Here. Take these. You'll forget,*
and I fall asleep standing and when I ride
passenger-side I open the door sometimes
instead of the window for a wake-up blast
and the doctor says,
No, absolutely never!
You would die for sure or kill someone.
Certainly can't drive now but this guy here
loves you, wants to help. Trust him.
No need to drive, work, think. Relax.
Everything is gonna be okay.

The Places Where Darkness Collects

For five hours Anne battles deluge,
fumbling for necessities: lights, fan, heater
in this borrowed car with a torn wiper
and a stubborn defog, zipped in on the right
by a plummet like the one that flattened Coyote
each childhood Froot Loop morning,
and on the left by trucks doing eighty.

Then FLASH! A rainbow lifts her
from the fading rain.

Anne exits for coffee, chicken-fried steak,

rhubarb pie and, breathing bolstered,
switch-backs again across the Appalachians
to love songs she's long ago laid down
and head-bobbing, non-drive foot tapping,
sings her wonder but the celebration slows
when in her periphery,
three muddy creeks smear her outlook.

This valley could envelop her if the sun
puts itself behind the mountains
before it delivers her to Morgantown.

Write me a poem, she coaxed, so...

I wrung out the pain of her birth
but that wasn't at all what she wanted.
She'd already borne enough sorrow
doled to her with hands dyed in blood.

I should have made her a mirror instead
to reflect the sky where her dreams lived
that beauty I noticed the first moment
but mistook for a mushrooming cloud.

I should have fashioned a torch for her fire
that some days burned more fierce than the sun.
She could carry it to light up dark corners
for those who lived hidden like her.

I should have crafted a room of petals
so she could sit silent with her dreams.
Then none could be crushed, so lovely
in this world that needs more like her.
Asleep love or should we talk?

And my jaws clamp safe-locked,
securing my secrets
but my teeth quake and my ears rumble,
even my breath lodges within
acute, jagged memories.

I fold their forms into origami fish,
plunging them beneath cenote* waters,
my own live offering
to the dreadful gods that torment me.

Rumbling, my neat creases unfold.
Fins flail and thrash, heaving the depths
where I've banished them,
creating a tsunami.
I scream, unable to quell their frenzy.

My lover strokes my hair, cooing
my cries into monologue,
fragmented images spoken aloud,
ricocheting sometimes until dawn.

*Cenote: a natural underground reservoir of water
such as occurs in the limestone of Yucatan, Mexico

Seasonal Changes

All of the Susans stand crowded
in their tattered yellow ribbons
and summer frocks.
Their numbers cry in unison
yet they murmur in a solitary voice,
black-faced, adoring the sun
with the joyous knowledge
that they own August's colors
regardless of October's fade.

Their songs spill over bending weeds,
every willow's tears scattered
like children near their feet.
Cedars stand guard, unconcerned
about changing seasons,
their garb lasting them year round.

Untouched by Earth's spin,
the zodiac brings nothing new
during passing months,
the trees' moods remain firm,
still, and strong.

Curb Appeal

She was new there, another addition
to the Elmwood sanitarium flow
as the gentry irons out the wrinkles,
this woman is old enough to remember
the chains, dank tunnels, fat needles
where now the corporation gilds
the outcast so tourists can turn terror
to fantasy, laying steep dollars down
for nights in a haunted castle.

Bewildered, she wanders wearing
fuzzy slippers, gown, terry robe.
So, offering bottled cold tea and pastry,
I cross over to her, but she has vanished,
that ghost of my long ago.
Yet the chill remains -
not just the damp that is Buffalo
during this strange El Niño winter,
but for the memory, naked and shivering,
awakened by a nightmare
in that solitary room.

She takes the haunted part of me
and returns at sunset.
I asked, *Do you live there?*
pointing, urging her to take shelter,

I don't want to talk, she says,

so I walk away,
retreading in the newly-poured cement
    the steps I'd made years before.

J. Tim Raymond

J. Tim Raymond has resided in Western New York since 1990. He grew up living in various towns around the United States and in Europe. He served in the Army during the Vietnam War before beginning a fine arts career in Baltimore, Washington D.C., New York, and Austin. Raymond exhibits paintings and performs as an actor in productions with the Subversive Theater Collective. His art reviews have appeared in *Artvoice* and *The Public*. He is a frequent reader at Buffalo poetry venues, and his short prose has been published in *A Flash of Dark* (The Writer's Den).

The Russian

I had dropped out of college after Thanksgiving and moved into a shared apartment in a suburb of DC, and joined a band. I was the only one there on New Year's Day. My roommate was with his girlfriend and her family in Georgetown. The other band members were with their families somewhere in the suburbs or tri-state area. A Russian woman in her forties who had recently moved in two doors down from me knocked on my door to ask if I would be going out. Would I buy her a pack of Camels? From all the typing I've heard, she was likely some kind of writer. Her clothes and jewelry suggested that she had--or once had--money. She looked a lot like the French actress,

Anouk Aimee. I told her I'd be happy to—figuring I might get to know her better.

I walked to the clutch of stores down the hill on Main Street in this little would-be-village to a 7-Eleven where I cashed checks. I bought a small rotisserie chicken, a six-pack of beer, the pack of Camels for her, Viceroys for me, and a small box of Whitman Samplers. Since we didn't have a phone at the apartment, the 7-Eleven took our calls or we just used the phone booth outside. I last used it to call my parents in Belgium on Christmas. After leaving the store, the phone in the booth rang. I let it go a few times while I lit a cigarette. What the hell, I picked up the receiver. It was the Russian telling me she left something at my door--just letting me know. She told me that she enjoyed meeting me. Odd, I thought, calling to tell me that.

Walking back up to the apartment by a different route, I stopped at a White Castle to buy a dozen sliders. It became cold since I left the apartment--didn't wear gloves, hat, or scarf. I quickened my pace. The Jehovah's Witnesses were out in force, bundled up in pairs, unfailingly cheerful. They nodded and wished me a Happy New Year. I nodded back, moving the sagging grocery bag from one arm to the other, stabbing my free hand deep in my jacket pocket for warmth.

A wailing siren cut through the misting early-afternoon chill of this quiet neighborhood of retired railroad workers, foreign students who didn't party, and civil service commuters like me. How urgent it sounded compared to the familiar ouh-wah-ouh-wah of the

European version. Feeling something in the pit of my stomach, I turned onto my street, slowed my pace, and watched as a police van with lights, but no siren, joined a bright growing swarm of patrol cars assembling at angles to the curb.

No note, nothing to give any impression things were going badly, nothing to indicate that on New Year's Day, 1967, the Russian woman would climb up to the roof of our four-story apartment house and jump off. Her embassy people arrived and questioned those of us still around.

"Do any of you know why she might have done this?"

I told them about the pack of Camels and her calling me at the store, telling me it was nice to have met me. Yes, I did think it was a bit strange, but not that strange. I didn't really know her. The embassy people chatted briefly with the cops. She had hit the snow bank behind the house. It wasn't deep enough to cushion the impact at all and underneath had been a large plastic swimming pool filled with old bicycles covered up by the piled drift. By the time they had extracted her remains and settled the initial inquiries, I was spent. The area of impact had been covered up with a giant black plastic tarp and marked off with sawhorses posting "Police Line - Do Not Cross." Crime scene or not, the next day a backhoe came and dumped the unholy mess into a truck.

After the cops left, I was still holding the sack of groceries—hadn't even been back to my apartment. I finally returned and found a box at my door— the kind that holds a ream of typing paper. Inside was a sauerkraut casserole, along with a small bottle of vodka. I took the box inside, holding it as a kind of reliquary. I put away the chicken, the sliders, and beer. My eyes locked onto a dinner knife, gelatinous with mayonnaise-smears on the bottom fridge tray, gleaming in a shallow pool of ice water.

I stared at it long and hard until the fridge motor jolted on.

I Got Out

"This is WZRO! Zorro Land Radio, coming to all y'alls up and down the coast from Jax Beach to St. Augustine, Florida. Let me know what you want to hear and I'll flip a platter for ya." That was the *platter patter* of Fred Butz, an AM radio DJ I went to school with in 1959.

He got off class early each Friday afternoon to do his radio show in this little seaside tourist town on the North Florida coast. Our institute of higher learning, which is what high school was called then, was Duncan U. Fletcher, named after a much-past governor of Florida and whose unofficial school motto was *Duncan U. Fletcher, Flunk'em U Betcha*. I was a year behind Fred in 8th grade. He was the *big man on campus*, a school celebrity. He did the morning announcements from the office PA. He was behind the mic at basketball games and MC'd the fundraiser for the pep club. I gaped at his hardy confidence with girls, his uncomplicated social charm. He was built chubby like an actor of the day, Allan Hale Jr. or maybe closer to Bill Haley. He had a cheery crinkle and mischievous twinkle in his eye. His favorite phrase was *not by a long shot.* He wore a black shirt and pants, with yellow socks and shiny black loafers.

I liked a girl who sat next to me in homeroom. Susie spoke to me about assignments, but after the bell, we went in different directions. She always wore a shirtwaist dress printed with household appliances or something. Girls still wore socks with loafers, even in Florida. Her hair was always up. I would see her at lunch with her friends, but never had the nerve to go sit with them. Susie's father owned the Shoreline Motel. I took swimming classes at the pool there. I saw her once in a pin-striped swimsuit and my crush got heavy. So it was a punch in the gut to see her walking out after school one Friday with Fred Butz. I stood sinking into the concrete as students broke field around me making their way to buses and cars. I could only see them from the back, but was sure it was Susie's blonde ponytail swishing down the wide school steps as they headed to the parking lot, to Fred's two-door '56 beige Renault Dauphine with white sidewalls. I heard the throaty roar of unmuffled tailpipes and the screech of tires on hot pavement as everybody drove to the A&W down the coast highway.

Because we were a Navy family, and my father always moved us into the community rather than live on the base, I always walked home, just a few blocks from school. At home, I stared into the cooling interior of the refrigerator imagining where and what Susie and Fred were going and doing and my cheeks burned. Out the window, I could see my mother finishing up hanging clothes on the line in the backyard. I closed the fridge and went to my room before she could ask me about my day. I switched on

WZRO. Fred's voice sounded even more resonant than usual, as if my would-be girlfriend was sitting on his lap at the radio station while he cued up Little Richard's *Tutti Frutti* for the tenth time in a row.

In my eighth grade year, my friends were mostly peripheral. Tommy Parrot was a good friend who played marathon Monopoly games with me the summer before. His father had taught me to water ski, but his Marine Dad had transferred after six months of the school year. Military families had short residencies, barely living in a place for two or three years. My father, a Navy aviator during the Cold War, flew home only a few times from his duty in the Arctic North. Sometimes I tagged along with two other boys from my class, Bonnie I. Smith and Hack Storms. With Bonnie standing at 6'4", and Hack at 5'2", they were like Mutt and Jeff, always together even though their fathers owned competing swimming pool supply stores. We mostly got along as equals, but on occasion, they would gang up and pointlessly tease me the entire school day.

In 1959, near the height of the Cold War, there were occasional Russian sub sightings off the coast by Ponte Vedra Beach. When the town air raid siren sounded, school would let out early. Everyone was supposed to get into their bomb shelters until the *all clear* signal. That was the idea anyway, but most everybody just drove to the beach. One Friday, close the end of the school year, the sirens went off and then the bells went off and the school patched into a bulletin from the radio. When a *Red* sub had been sighted off the coast, two jets at the carrier base at Mayport scrambled to investigate. Some people took the sub sightings as the coming of the Apocalypse.

As I was getting my gym stuff from my locker to head out the main door, Fred Butz put a hand on my shoulder to invite me to join his friends to go to the A&W, a favorite drive-in root beer stand where Fred held court, taking record requests and gathering gossip before his show. Stupidly flattered, I piled into the Renault with two of his basketball buddies in the back. We barely fit into the back seat of that little Renault. That left the front passenger side open. I was certain who was going sit there. Susie bounded to the car waving to her jealous friends, and gave Fred a proprietary kiss on the cheek. She nodded at the team players in the back and fired an additional glance at me as she snuggled close to Fred. As Fred accelerated onto the main road, two F-11-F Cougar jets streaked overhead, towards the beach.

Not wishing to follow the developments in the front seat any further, I said, "Thanks Fred, I'll just walk home from here."

My ears still ringing from the flyover, I repeated, "Hey Fred, I said I'll just get out here and walk home," but he drove right through the intersection.

When he didn't respond, I repeated my desire to get out of the car. Instead, he turned up the radio to hear Buddy Holly's *Peggy Sue.*

"Let me out, Fred!" I shouted.

Fred finally pulled over.

"Okay, okay….get out for Christ's sake."

The basketball player moved to let me slide out the passenger front. I broke free from my awkward exit glancing at the girl who held the back of her seat with one hand to let me out, while with the other, she lit Fred's Lucky. The car door slammed shut with a ringing finality. The Dauphine had a city horn and country horn. I got two beeps of the country horn as Fred pulled back into traffic.

By the time I got back home, the all clear siren had sounded. I threw my gym stuff into the wash sink and went into my room to fume and sulk. I looked down and saw my brand spanking new chinos had an ink stain.

Fred's show was about to broadcast. Just to further punish myself, I turned on the radio, but it wasn't Fred's voice. It was another news announcer at the mic speaking in clear stentorian tones.

"Not an hour ago, WZRO's own personality, Fred Butz, was injured in a car accident on Coast Drive. His three passengers were also seriously hurt. All were taken by ambulance to Duvall County Hospital. We will keep you informed as we know more. At this critical time, our hearts and prayers are with these young people, families, and friends."

My mother, who also heard the announcement, came into my room.

"Oh, those kids! It's just horrible. Did you know them? You knew that boy with the radio show, didn't you-- Zorro—was that his name? Oh, the poor parents!"

My hearing mind had turned off. I could only stare at my mother's mouthings. In my head were words I would never say to her. *I got out.*

My mind reeled at the chance whims of the universe. I later learned that the '56 Renault was designed so that in the event of a crash, the windows pop out. But without seatbelts, so did passengers. Fred's car hit the only non-palm tree on Seabreeze Boulevard and Atlantic Coast Highway. Fred remained seated as the steering wheel pushed into his chest, crushing his windpipe and puncturing his lung. He died at the scene.

The boys were thrown from the car, one, who catapulted over Fred out the driver's side door, was paralyzed from the waist down. The other, who was ejected out the back window, was able to reconstruct the impact to the police as he had his head stitched up.

Susie, hit the windshield and went through it. She endured much facial reconstruction, and ultimately healed up pretty well, considering she had been thrown onto the crumpled hood of the car.

The whole school and most of the town came to Fred's wake held at the beach at the time of his three o'clock radio show. A biplane normally used for crop dusting flew over the wave tops about a hundred yards out towing a banner spelling WZRO as Fred's ashes were spread with the incoming tide.

Rev. Barry Abraham Zavah

Barry Zavah is a 72 year-old an expatriate WNYer, a retired Erie County Assistant DA, an ordained minister, Reiki Master. He has been an RVer since 12/2002, full-time since 12/2007. He made Alpine-Big Bend Texas his home in 2008.

His articles and columns have appeared in *Sierra Club Big Bend Chapter*, *Border Hotline News*, *La Voz*, *Alpine Daily Planet*, *Alpine "o6" Cowboys*, *Pecos League of Professional Baseball*, and stories in *Chaos – A Journal of Texas Mountain Trail Writers*, *Annual West Texas Writers' Anthology*, Kay Kennedy's *Looking Back: Boomers Remember History*. He has written guest columns in *Big Bend Sentinel*, and letters to the editor, frequently published in Alpine-Big Bend regional newspapers and across Texas\.

Around and About the Big Bend
aided by the Astute Editorial Assistance of Alicia Trillo

South County Run

Rather than responding in a terse manner to ill-informed judgments from *certain* readers' concerning my letters to the editor and misleading, political memes from social media trolls, it was time for *Ishmael's* way. We creative breeds can identify with that.

For example, how about when the best piece of literature submitted for publication since the modern English alphabet married the word processor, walked down the aisle by auto correct, gets a spate of rejections? How about another's innocent enough critique at a writer's group meeting? How about the pot luck dinner when overhearing some culinary boor's distasteful remark about your best recipe?

Doors #1, 2 and 3 for me, Monty!

In response, "… *especially whenever my hypos get such an upper hand of me, that it requires a strong moral principle to prevent me from deliberately stepping into the street, and methodically knocking people's hats off*" the ways of the world brings me to identify with Ishmael's sense of things. I'm sufficiently aware of the *hat-knocking* part that it troubles me enough to do something more constructive.

So, by mid-February of the Year of Our Lord's consternation with the on-going national state of things, making it incredibly easy to push our buttons, it was nigh past time for Alicia and me to take to the '85 Toyota Supra and reconnect with Big Bend. Another compelling motive was to see the blue bonnets along FM 170.

Though early in the season, they were abundant in longer, larger, more glorious State flower patches than seen before. We capped a wonderful day with an excellent dinner at the Starlight Theatre in Terlinqua.

February 2019 marked the 16th anniversary of finding Alpine-Big Bend in my first RV travel season. The people were a major factor, but I fell hard for the region at the Madera Canyon Overlook west of the Lajitas Resort. Here, the narrow road drops out of the mountains following the course of the Rio Grande west to Presidio, a border crossing city into Mexico.

I'd never seen anything like this in all my 55 northeast years. At that elevation the river was as wide as my thumb at arm's length. Humidity contained within the canyon produced a primordial mist that painted landscape vegetation a lush green. The late afternoon's mid-winter sun highlighted textures and revealed colors among a wealth of minerals embedded in ancient mountain walls.

There's a treasure chest of magnificent enough to open the senses and heal the spirit along the border. For *"driving off the spleen, and regulating the circulation"*, a South County run does *Ishmael's* justice for me.

Summer of '63

The following story came to mind when going through an inventory of possibilities for a submission to the *Chaos Anthology*. Placed between the two involving Big Bend, I suppose it delineates my rebirth here after my life in my Buffalo NY birthplace.

In 1963, a nasty summer storm inundated North Buffalo basements and streets with brackish, brown-green liquid 'stuff'. That morning with my friends I watched a VW Beetle pull to the water's edge of a flooded viaduct, it's depth but a couple inches from the bottom of the twin railroad trestles spanning Delaware Avenue three blocks north of my Stratford Road home.

The driver stopped, got out and walked to the waters' edge. Probably weighing all his options, the pluses and minuses, of driving through the deep water, he said "How do I get from here to …?"

Great question! He must have been a college graduate. Undeterred by the magnitude of the challenge, likely with his own spleen to sooth, he returned to his car. Moving forward a few inches, he paused, then onward in his *Man of La Mancha* quest with destiny, confronted the heaviest rain storm in 15 years, one overwhelming the Sewer Authority's resources. Sure enough, the VW completely disappeared under the murky depths.
"Glug, glug, glug!" Giant air bubbles rose to the surface followed by Mr. Unlucky. I was glad that he could swim because I dare say, few of us would come to his rescue in the middle of "water most foul".

At some point the floods receded, and our teenage boys' summer of 1963 lives continued with our dysentery-free dilemmas. Pre-learner's permit driver's license, we bicycled all over the place. We would ride to the nearby Comet Cone Company for scraps of broken cones. Bowling? Softball? Play Monopoly or Risk on a front porch? A double feature downtown, followed by a visit to the used comic book store on Chippewa Avenue and two slices of Dino's pizza before grabbing the Delaware Avenue bus and heading home?

Did that flooded viaduct, challenged by a bug, prepare me for a retiree's peaceful life in remote Far West Texas? No, but it certainly made that day live forever.

The Common Thread

Not to be ignored is the 74 mile Davis Mountains Scenic Loop, about 106 miles north of the Study Butte TX 118/ FM 170 junction in South County to Ft. Davis and another 53 miles to I-10.

In several of my early years in Big Bend, before departing for an extended RV travel season, I'd treat myself to one last magnificent romp and a large offering of crisp mountain air. It had to hold me until returning four to seven months later.

Likely from honoring the gods a day or two before, we had a mid-April snowfall. The two dry creek beds past the McDonald Observatory were running wild, cold water from on high pursued by the sun's warming rays. I stopped my RAV4 in the middle of the first creek, opened all four windows and sunroof to breathe it all in and be one with nature. Ahhhh!

Alpine-Big Bend became "official" in March, 2008. The original owners of Murphy's knew something about that. They had a pizzeria in Ft. Davis when I stopped there for lunch in February 2003 before heading to the McDonald Observatory.

Mr. Murphy shared a now-familiar story.

"We came out here (from Chicago), saw the mountains, got on the phone to family and friends and told them 'Pack us up and send it here. We're *not* coming back'."

The far West Texas wilderness beckons you back if you experience it once. A new person may emerge to enjoy a life poles apart from those big city days. Amen for that common thread.

Scott Williams

Dr. Scott Williams as a SUNY Buffalo Professor Emeritus was nationally honored as one of the top 50 research scientists and received the SUNY Chancellor's Award for Excellence in Teaching. Since his 2013 SUNY retirement, Scott has become a poet and author of short stories. His poetry has appeared in fourteen journals and newspapers, for example, *Punch Drunk Press*, *Peach Mag, Juniper, Night and Day, Owl Light News*, and *The Buffalo News*. Most recent of his books are "*Bonvibre Haiku*" (CWP Press-2017), "*Natural Shrinkage*" (Destitute Press-2018), "*A Flash of Dark*" (Writers Den-2018) and "*A Flash of Dark* Vol. 2*"* (Writers Den-2018). Williams co-hosts the series Second Stage Writers and also Poets Soup.

Acknowledgements

"Half Not Twice" appeared in *Night and Day* 2016, "Long Legged Susan, My Lover" appeared in *The Buffalo News* 2017, Hot Dog Delights" appears in *Le Mot Juste* 2018

hot dog delights

I was glad when my mother's day was filled with music or meetings cause it was always *hot dogs* between Dad and me. Eating out or him cooking at home *hot dogs* skinless or with the well-done natural casing crunchy skin-on texture; *hot dogs* with mustard, or ketchup and/or relish from the Pennsylvania Dutch; *hot dogs* with plain white rolls or sour dough rolls or whole grain rolls; *hot dogs* with sauerkraut with or without mayonnaise or sautéed peppers and onions; *hot dogs* with ground beef and a side of onion rings.

In college, it was reverence eating *hot dogs* cooked in beer, ale or stout, or with chili powder. A late night meal of *hot dogs* smothered in bacon or bacon bits or topped with fava beans, pinto beans, tomato vinaigrette, mashed potato, canned corn and jalapeño salsa. Yes, it was like **Kama-dog-Sutra**, the **Kama Sutra** of *hot dogs*, trying food positions, we enjoyed it every way without or with Swiss or Muenster or Camembert or Cheese Whiz. And our taste for *hot dogs* expanded to wursts: Knockwurst and Knackwurst and Bratwurst.

In stores now, *hot dogs* are all beef, or mixed pork and beef, all veal or mixed pork and veal. Popular with kids is pizza stuffed in *hot dogs* or *hot dogs* on pizza. In suburbia discover the new "Fish dogs," *hot dogs* topped with calamari, clams, lobster, mussels or salmon and a butter sauce. Diets around the world demand availability of turkey dogs or camel dogs or veggie dogs.

In the end, the overwhelming extras give witness to our slurping, grinding, popping, sucking and suckling sauces delightfully dribbling down our throats disguising *our hot dogs*.

This a warning

I'm gonna read here today.
I'm gonna read and read here today.
I'm gonna read and read and read
and read and read and read
and read here today.
I'm gonna read beyond sipped java.
Read beyond drowsy eyes.
Read beyond too long.
Read beyond presidential lies.
Read so long you'll be pleased I forgot my hot dog poem.
Read so long I'll be in your dreams reading.
Read until you think we're married and ask for divorce.
Read so long that stopping and starting are the same.
Read so long that you will forget and remember and forget
    and remember and forget again and ...
    hate my name.

RIGHT NOW   I   amm   gonnaa   reeead   1001
    ovvvv   myyy   faaaavoooriiiite   slooow
    meeeeeterrrrrr   poems.

Patio Boys

Jeopardy winner professionals, aged forty, fifty, and sixty.
Mesmerized with drool by tasty yoga pants or tight shorts
and tee-shirts.

They are three smoking Camels and drinking coffee at a
    Buffalo café.
taking one black, one two sugars, one his skin color.

Not Starbucks, Dunkin D's, nor Timmy H's awnings
restrict tan from one hundred and fifty-year-old bald heads.

across Elmwood Avenue from Rite Aid or
the Big Four Cleaners or No Name Bar or across
Main Street from Lake Effect Diner or the Cantalician
    School.

They are three smoking Camels and drinking Columbian at
    a Buffalo café.

One man, lamenting a relationship bereft of sex, wishes for
    piety leaking from the corner of his eyes.
One man is on-the-run from a stunning-man-eating tigress
    and has humble-veneered- stupid-belying brilliance.
One man pines after she who left his millions for another,
    yet has the occasional dung in his briefcase.

They are three smoking Camels and drinking Jamaican at a
    Buffalo café.

Dearly desiring companionship, longing to fill
imagined pedestals without depression and pills,
they drink and inhale vehicle particulates on patios.

As boasting books one has read gives way to
politics one has heard, gives way to philosophy
one conjectures, gives way to proofs and facts, they laugh

*while smoking Camels and drinking Kenyan at a Buffalo
    café.*

One day a tall mid-twenties Japanese beauty,
enthralled by their humor and converse,
sits at the table with adoring eyes wide and

*now, four are smoking Camels and drinking Turkish at that
    Buffalo café.*

The musketeers treat her to lunch and a movie.
Though at conclusion, each is unhappy that she sees
only friendship from three tired old men.

Without dinner, without alcohol, without companionship,
they drive late model cars to quiet homes and
memories of a she with a towering imagined pedestal.

Soon the youngest is left only prayer, by brain-muzzling
    cancer.
The eldest's Alzheimer's fizzles away in depression.
And now there is but one, alone with his poetry,

Smoking Camels and drinking coffee at a Buffalo café.

Half Not Twice

I lived in fear of dying
before my time,
a fading shadow
in friends' memories.

And so I worked thirty years
nightly sleeping but five hours
as if I might live twice the life
of the napping ordinary man.

And it was fun doing math,
creating art, playing jazz,
dancing in the clubs of life
between rain drops and family.

And at fifty-eight spared heart
attack but not a stroke slowing
the mighty asking "Do you want
ordinary life in half the time?"

And I was reminded of forgotten
hunger for an extraordinary wish
hunger for something special must be
filled inside, not drizzled outside.

Long Legged Susan, My Lover

That summer on The Farm was hot and wet.
Fly strips had "full, no vacancy" signs.
The pond had peepers, frogs and green scum.
Night sky was a thrill of new-to-me stars.

A hurricane remnant passed through.
Lightning struck the huge tree near the pond.
Soon there were tsunamis of mosquitoes.
The annoyances thought me a chocolate sundae.

Yes, flies serenaded the meeting hall,
landing on arms, legs and face yet,
mosquitoes held chomp court there,
persistent whines in my ear and bites on skin.

My personal space was found in the big house,
up the creaking ladder from second floor west,

in eight four-by-eight spaces plus two with windows,
at night, made ten supposedly livable breezeless spaces.

Surrounding each space, was nylon netting
from floor to slanted attic ceiling.
Yet, despite one's agility, myriads of mosquitoes
had dinner invitations to accompany you to bed.

You might smack a dozen before sleep,
but in the morning your forehead, neck,
exposed arms received bumps on their bumps.
Mindfulness to mosquitoes? I hated the damn things.

I don't know why I let long-legged Susan stay
that first night that I met her, but next morning
I had only five bumps,
the second night only one bump.
Afterwards, thanks to long-legged Susan, none.

Susan and I were fast friends that summer,
her protection from annoyances supreme.
I henceforth named all spiders Susan.
Again I could pretend mindfulness to bugs.

I Did Not Do Your Homework

The dog ate it and I tried it again,
on that one, my roommate spilled beer again.
The wind blew away the third try again.
And so, I did not do YOUR homework.

Grandma's famous potato salad is rich,
with bacon, avocado, and lutefisk.
The warm mayonnaise made everyone ill.
And so I did not do YOUR homework.

Oh, and the weed was a good high, Sir,
but it was laced with horse tranquilizer.
I slept sixteen hours through two alarms,
And so I did not do YOUR homework.

My boyfriend… the man I was to marry,
oh that jerk spent the night with my best friend.
You bet I camped the night by that whore's door.
And so I did not do YOUR homework.

No, I wasn't at the Ebony Fashion Fair
I was the driver for Miss Bermuda,
and Miss Ohio, who asked me inside-oh!
And so I did not do YOUR homework.

I was driving home when I freaked,
parade of police cars passed by me, to
break on some poor soul their Billy clubs.
And so I did not do YOUR homework.

Last night I made a beer run to 7-11.
Three guys tried to mug **ME**, a Special Forces
Vet. Two I hurt real bad and killed the third.
And so I did not do YOUR homework.

For how many years have you given this
routine, emotionless, boring assignment.
I see no reason to waste a day so very fine.
And so I did not do YOUR homework.

After Grandpa's funeral my sleepy
brother drove Mom's two fathers home.
I drove Mom and Dad while brother crashed.
And so I did not do YOUR homework.
Students, I ask the rest of you, why *YOU didn't complete
the assignment.*

Ghazal: A Shot in the I, again

With frequency, an ophthalmologist puts a needle in my
eye to reduce swelling in a cornea.
As the swollen dam in Johnstown burst, Andrew Carnegie
said,
"Down through the chasm the wild waves flew."

Swimming with snakes is akin to apprenticing a politician.
In their water,
political snakes have claws.
Upon each return to Baltimore, I seek the best crabs to eat.
Until I caught one.
Now I am celibate.

I never knew celibacy was a part of marriage, but for some
it is a delayed wedding vow.
I never felt so enthused by a pope as the present one.
He could even learn from the Dalai Llama.

Scott, could a neurologist give you a shot in the head to
transfer the swelling from ego to the land of the silent.

Ghazal: Left Freezer Open

I left the freezer door open. Everything is thawed or melted.
I left the stove burner on, and the bottom of the pot is crust.

Your red automobile starts keyless, warms inside
This stanza from the last models the automobile.

All beef hot dogs sir, please, well-done with fries and
    onion rings to stuff a Friday dinner for us two.

Those five young girls exhibit beauty's negation carelessly

Walking in the street unhinges the old man's peeking.

Five houses down dwells the aged eighty Japanese bride,
Of a deceased American husband, in a bonsai home

The Japanese woman daily walks two miles to grocery.
Gone
Are offspring. She carts home vegetables, fish and rice for
one.

The aged eighty widow has better health to burn
ten years your junior, her brain remains strong
    Your memory's onion peels and burns your I.

The Music House

For Beryl E. Williams   1913-1999

Age five outside
apartment window
playing in the mud
some on fingers,
some in mouth.
Dirt on clothes,
dirt in hair.
Making cakes and pies.
I hear the scale:
C,D,E,F,G,F,E,D,C
D,E,F,G,A,G,F,E,D
E,F,G,A,B,A,G,F,E.

Mother's notes going
up and down and
my fingers feel that
up and down and

both hands one
with exercising
our fingers.

Then kneeling,
fingers spread,
in mud or dirt
with thirteen
pebble keys,
I press piano with her
on the stones.
Khachaturian's *Sabre Dance,*
Mozart's *Turkish Dance,*
Chopin's *Fantasie Impromptu,*
Brahms' *Waltz in A Flat,*
Grieg's *March of the Dwarfs.*
Playing with her our favorites.

Mom told me stories/symphonies
I fell in love with her piano's
Prokofiev's *Love for Three Oranges:*
Dah-dah-dah-dah-da-dadah,
da-dadah da-dadah da-dadah.

In the mud and on my pebble piano
I played for and
I told my friend Milton
of Prokofiev's *Peter and the Wolf*
Mussorgsky's *Night on Bald Mountain,*
and Stravinsky's *Firebird.*

Seventy years later
I still carry
tales of Prince Ivan's
riding across seven lands,
sailing over seven seas

to meet the Grey Wolf,
to find the Firebird,
to steal the Firebird,
to meet the Golden Mane Horse,
to steal the Golden Mane Horse,
to meet Helen the beautiful,
to marry Helen the beautiful.

Just outside the window
riding the Grey Wolf,
playing in mud, dirt, and stones,
making pies and playing piano.

A Shock for Aged

It can come as a shock when
  people are always referring to you as *sir*.
  vacant seats are offered and doors held open.
  beautiful women only kiss your crown.
  your wisdom is more from experience than
      intelligence.
  massage is the best thing you have felt in years.
  the frequency of lost items accelerates.
  unknown white women are no longer frightened by
      you.
  very small amounts of food fill you.
  daily bathroom visits quadruple.
  you forget to zip up your pants.
  you forget to zip down your pants.
It can come a deep shock
when you appreciate feeling shocks.

Michael Zanolli

Michael Zanolli lived for many years in Seoul, South Korea where he taught at Yonsei University. At night, he played in a series of bands at the legendary Just Blues club. He is currently running out of money in Buffalo, NY.

After Seeing *The Fog of War* With a Friend

After the film,
Drinking coffee on a cloudy day,
Pondering quietly.

No one speaks. Both of us
Numb to the question despite the coffee.
Each of us remains silent,

Stoking old resentments.
My eye fixed on a distant factory
In some third world backwater.

You, dreaming of a stream
Of products flowing west, like rare objects
In the intellect of God.

But behind the silence
Lines of force are drawn. Vague allegiances…
Lines in drifting sand.

It was you broke the silence:
"He spent his whole life doing good to
To make it up." Full stop.

I felt it as a challenge,
But demurred. What did you know about it?
Yet it rankled. Who were you

To judge? (And who was I?)
And yet I, confronted by this fact,
Could not, it must be said,
Bring myself to differ.
How should I explain myself to her?

(Who knew beyond a certainty

The goodness of our leaders --
Something to be taken for granted).
I sat silent,

Wrapped in my indifference.
I stirred my coffee and watched the clouds
Revolve like galaxies.
Cold and the cryptic clouds
Kept me, poor sinner, from seeing straight.
I focused on the coffee,

The clouds, and the cold.
It must have been an hour or two later
That I ventured something.

But she had since moved on,
And whatever it was I managed
Didn't amount to squat.

Untitled

Outside, winter's bluster
Makes havoc of our wintry daydreams
And generates uncertainty.
Here, for the moment, I
(The heat turned up, National Grid be damned),
Pursue my toothless plan.

If, at the age of twelve,
I stood on tiptoe, tiny hands outstretched,
Reaching for the topmost

Shelf of the tall bookcase,
Where, among other tomes my mother
Hoped to hide a fugitive

Lust, or so I thought,
One big book in particular caught
My eager roving eye:

Butler's *The Way of All Flesh*.
Misunderstanding "the way," I sought
To comprehend its meaning,

Well, otherwise. This mistake,
Confusing what I thought was dawning
Sexual awareness,

With, well, death, would dog me
As an idea until years later
(It should be understood

I'm speaking tongue-in-cheek)
When experience would set me straight

(When "the way" was Revealed)
Now, I stand by the window
And stare – it's really coming down out there -
Raise a fist in defiance.

Age lodges its protest.
I continue the quest (the crusade)
For a little warmth.

Voices

At breed in a tired brain,
Just out of shot of hearing, voices
Prattling on about nothing.
Half asleep, you lie there in the dark,
Listening, listening…
Not even voices, really; just sounds
Vaguely human; birds even.

All the sounds that things make:
The maddening ringing in one's ears;
Remembered rush of wind
And dead leaves in a tremulous puddle;
Or as you lie half asleep in bed,
The dull drone of the bedroom heater.
The world of sound around.

And behind and beyond
Each thing with its sound, there are voices
That talk of the weather,
Or call your name as a mother might,
Back when you were little.
But it's mostly innocuous nonsense,

Blank chatter of strangers.

And they push you through your pain,
Or rather, the fact that you hear them,
That you know how to listen,
How to hear what that everyday world
Of everyday noises
Conceals - this fact somehow comforts you,

As if you were special.
And because of this fact,
In some way that you don't understand,
They help you with the pain -
Though not to make it any smaller --
The pain is all you have.

Number Eleven
This always cracked us up;
Jeff doing the scratchy Shakespeare record:
To-morrow, and to-morrow,

And to-morrow, creeps in
This petty pace from day to day,"
As if he were a crow.

That was so long ago,
And so much (dirty) water has flowed
Under the proverbial bridge

That I can't help feeling
(These days it's so much pie-a-la-mode,
This feeling that I'm getting old)

Like something kept in the fridge
To be consumed on a rainy day.
More to the point is this:

Foul whisp'rings are abroad.
This morning's newspaper spills
Through the eyes of the Toad.

Each day outdoes the last.
Each day some new, scandalous outrage
Knocks at our silent hearts.

Cold weather and chattering
Birds chasten a weathered moral sense,
A time, then, of terrible waste.

We await some saint-of-the-impossible
Who will offer us an angel and
The sure touch of a king.

But such thoughts disappear
Before the battle with my family.
Family trumps the Toad.

Number Twelve
This fascinating thing:
Hauling ancient recollections out
Of the memory hole

And bringing them into the light.
Sauerkraut's sour taste depends on
Its sugar-eating soul.

One night, Jesse and I.
The best of friends, took in a show:
A droll piece about class.

My illness, as always,
Though it did not preclude the outing,
Alas, ruled out concentration.

In a daze, in a whirl,
The shouting on the stage in my ears,
The situation desperate,

The girl on stage visionary,
The father who has given up beer,
The mother who must wait.

Nary a word was spoken
About my fateful illness.
The fear I felt, the dread.

Michael Delaney

Michael Delaney is a Professor of Mathematics at Erie Community College and an officer in the faculty union - he also runs ECC's professional development. He has written fiction and poetry for 23 years but has been remarkably unprolific. He has published in the *Buffalo News*, *ArtVoice*, and two anthologies, Gary Earl Ross' *Nickel City Nights*, and Scott Williams' *A Flash of Dark II*. He is cofounder, with George Grace, of the LitGarden Writers group which is now over 11 years old. He lives in Hamburg, NY with his wife Judy Stenroos, a retired Buffalo Kindergarten teacher. He has one son, Ivan.

Chino

Chino smelled like horses
when I was a kid.
Lots of skinny men
Chicano and Anglo
sported straw cowboy hats
sunburns
string ties
with longhorn clasps
drove Ford Rancheros
with one bale of hay in the back
under the serene watch
of the three San Gabriels.

The State Prison is in Chino
as you know.
So was the State Hospital
where my parents worked
for a while.

I don't know what's there now.
We lived there '55 – '59
then moved (most of us)
down to Costa Mesa
which smelled like the ocean.
Mom was gone

by May '61.
After school was over
Dad moved us all in
with his girlfriend and her two
strange little girls
back in Chino
way out of town
for a while.

One summer day
out in the yard
I saw the weeds rippling
smelled something
halfway between
hot electric motor
and powdered shit.
Grabbed it.
Knew the species:
green garter snake
skinny but long
five feet.
I knew something
about reptiles

If you don't grab them
right behind the head
they turn fast and bite.
It did.

Went and told my Dad
showed him the snake
and the bite.

No fang marks.
He said, *Let's check this out*
slowly got up
searched the bookshelf for my
Field Guide to North American Reptiles
leafed through it an ungodly long time.
At last he said

That was a Cottonmouth Moccasin.

He went to the Frigidaire
cracked open another Lucky Lager

sat back in his Lazy Boy
lit up an L&M
smiled to himself
and found the page
where he had stopped reading his

stinking
Earl
Stanley
Gardner
paperback.

Time's Arrow

I woke up with the idea
that all the wine we drank together
came back out of our bodies
flesh to blood to belly to gullet
regurgitated into crystal one sip at a time
bottles happily reassembled from
their smashed remains
in the green and brown glass bins
came home to syphon the wine from our two glasses
(yours and mine), recorked, resealed,
restocked on shelves,
repacked in cartons, reloaded in truck trailers,
warehouses, airfreight containers
the bellies of backwards-flying airplanes,
repatriated to Europe, South America, Australia
where, juvenated in barrels, engorged in winepresses,
    sheathed in grape skins
attached to vines and sucked down into the ground
it sleeps in the sun-warmed soil
fitfully, heart beating,
awaiting resurrection.

Candy Hearts

Too sexy for kids,
too uncool for teenagers;
the candy with no demographic.

Who are they for?
Mushy old people?
Curly-headed cartoon kids
whose closing kiss
balloons into a giant heart,
engulfing them both like the Blob?
Calico cuties
and boys in overalls?
Sentimental boys
who would never delight
in terrorizing the herds of pony girls?

They were disgusting
but we ate them like handfuls
of bad TV shows.

They used to say things like:
1.   23 SKIDOO and
2.   OH YOU KID.
3.   Honest.

In our twenties
we sowed our wild candy hearts
strewing pink BE MINEs
and purple KISS MEs
heedlessly in our paths.

If they made them
with different messages
like WHAT HAPPENED?
Y NOT ME?
U FELT THE SAME
NEVER FRIENDS

HOPE U SUFFER
U'LL B SORRY
BAD 4 EVER
ANGRY
SAD
JEALOUS
I HATE U
not to give away
but just to eat
to take and break and
crunch and mix
with saliva and
let them run sweetly
down our throats;
to incorporate the words
metabolize them
into something healthful
but soundless
and without power
instead of letting them rule
and torture us,
then these little pills
would soothe
and console
and have some purpose
at last.

Pamela

Pamela walks into the cemetery through an archway of enormous trees. She knows words, not trees. They could be oaks, chestnuts, maples, sycamores. They are big and green and dark. The midsummer light is fading fast, but at eight in the evening daylight still lingers. She reaches into her jean jacket pocket and pulls out the joint Tommy mailed her. It's probably been two years since she's smoked, maybe longer. She wants to feel like herself again.

She walks past a group of people gathered at a plot with maybe a dozen headstones enclosed in a wrought iron fence. They are getting ready to leave, slowly boarding a small yellow school bus. They are all women and girls – with all different colors of hair, mostly long, lots of braids. Black and white women and girls together. Each one is wearing a white or pastel-colored dress - frilly, feminine, old fashioned. Pamela imagines they are wearing petticoats. Who wears petticoats? Just came from a church service? Church service on a weekday evening in mid-summer? Is this a religious holiday? Anniversary of somebody's death? Pamela feels severed from her own time. She wants a sensible explanation for all this but can't think of one. What's going on here? Why are they so quaint? Why no men? No boys? The whole thing is disturbing.

Pamela walks a long way up the hill past the women and girls. She turns and watches as they all climb into the yellow bus, chirping like chickadees, and it rolls slowly down the hill, until it turns out of the cemetery, headlights briefly illuminating scenes of the main road, and then is gone. No one is around now.

She pulls her Zippo lighter out of her back jeans pocket and lights up a blunt, taking a big hit. It tastes good, smells good, mild - she was afraid she would cough. A reunion with her old drug of choice. She scans the cemetery again just to make sure she's alone. Nobody. Light is fading fast. The days when a cop car pulling onto the cemetery road would have sent her scampering to hide behind a tombstone are long gone, but old reflexes die hard. She is feeling just a little tense but still good.

She takes another pull and continues her walk up the hill, joint still burning. She's slowing down. The big trees silhouetted against the sky look really vivid. She stops and leans on a tree, taking in the scene, takes a deep breath of summer trees and cemetery flowers and soil, and considers her next move. Maybe one more hit and put it out, you don't know how strong this stuff is. This is the *clinical stuff*. Be careful – you're not used to it. She takes one more big toke. She lets it out slowly. No problem. She stubs the joint out on the tree, slips it in her jacket pocket despite the stink, and continues up the hill.

Suddenly it hits her. She is thinking about Jack and Molly. Damn it. She hasn't expected this. And it's clear she hasn't dealt with it. She hasn't felt it. And here it comes – her ex-husband is now with her longtime best friend, her post-separation lover. The intensity of the pain surprises her. This is much worse than when she found out. Oh, shit. What was she thinking? Did she think being strong means you never have to suffer?

What did they do together? Unfortunately right now she can visualize every possible scene in wide-screen Technicolor. Molly said they ran into each other by accident *in fucking Trader Joe's for Christ's sake* and both realized how much they loved Pamela and they spontaneously had a big hug and a cry. And then? Did they go right back to Molly's place and fuck each other's eyeballs out until they were comatose, to console themselves for breaking Pamela's fucking heart, both of them, in the worst possible way? Stomped it in the dirt! Those pieces of shit! The ultimate twisting of the knife. Oh, Jesus, this hurts so bad!

Pamela is doubled over as if gut shot, leaning on a big tree's exposed root. Then she looks up.

There are three figures standing at the top of the hill silhouetted against the twilight sky. Tall and massive. Freakishly so.

They just stand there. Pamela is not sure they are real. She believes they are looking at her. She slides out of the line of sight behind the tree, hunkers down in the dirt, and keeps on watching. The figures continue slowly down the path making low animal noises. Their grunts echo.

Pamela is convinced they know where she is. Her heart is pounding hard and fast. She frantically searches her vicinity for a big stick to use as a weapon. She spots one about ten feet down the hill from her and she crawls backwards on her belly through the dirt and clutches it tightly to her. What did Danny say that one time? You go for the biggest one and you hit him as hard as you can. Then you run like hell before the others have time to react. Have your route planned – the fastest way to where the people and cars are. Make a big scene. Don't yell rape, yell fire. That's what you do. You don't worry about hurting the big one – smash his head in if necessary. It's you or them. Suddenly she is ready for them. Terror has turned into resolve. *Come on, motherfuckers.*

Pamela watches them for what seems like forever, clutching her stick with sweaty hands and hardly breathing. The three figures slowly descend the hill, passing out of view behind the big trees. Finally their shadows emerge into the clearing next to her tree. Then their bodies emerge. Three skinny teenaged boys dressed in shorts and t-shirts. They smell like cigarettes and acrid boy sweat. One is talking on his cell phone.

He says, "We're just going over to Sam's house, Mom. We'll call you when we get there." He takes a drag on his cigarette. He has red hair and a Metallica shirt. His friends chuckle.

"Yeah, okay, no, we're sleeping over at Sam's. You can call Sam's mom."

"Okay, we're just gonna play video games in the basement and eat popcorn. Denise said it was okay. They have tons of sleeping bags"
'Yeah, we'll be fine. I'll call you tomorrow morning before I go to school. Yeah, we can shower. Love you, Mom."
One friend can no longer contain his mirth and lets out a big guffaw. Pamela considers jumping up, baring teeth and claws, and screaming like a panther. It would be so great. They would absolutely shit themselves if she got it exactly right. She doesn't do it. She's disappointed in herself. She lies down flat and starts breathing normally.

The taller friend says, "So Emma's parents aren't coming home."
"Statement or question?" asks the redhead.
"That's what you said."
"Yeah that's what she told me. You brought the handcrafted, fair trade, free-range vodka?"
"If that's what you wanna call it. Jamie charged me twenty but I know it's like eight ninety-nine a quart."

"And you say Emma'll pull the train for us if we get her juiced up fast enough?"

"Bobby said she sucked off half a dozen college guys after she got wasted at that big post-game party at the Statesman. In the back room. I don't know for sure that happened. But I'm ready just in case."

"You brought the paper bag with the hole in it?"

They all crack up. The sound of their barking laughter makes Pamela want to puke.

The other friend says, "I smell weed."

"Yeah, you definitely smell, pal," the redhead says. "Let's get out of here. It's creepy." They move on.

Pamela thinks: *Criminals. Little fucking slimebucket would-be rapists. I should call the cops.*

Then she thinks: *Maybe not. I don't know who they are or where they're going and I will just get into the shit myself. I'll be fucked and the cops won't even bother with these kids.*

The girl will probably throw up and pass out quickly. Those little shits will get scared and run home.

Jesus, I hope so.

Josh Smith

If your name was "Josh Smith," you'd try to set yourself apart, too. You'd ride motorcycles to the stage, set fire to objects while there, maybe bring a bullhorn or two just for insurance.

And if you were from Buffalo, New York, you'd try to punch above your weight. You might travel and perform across the country, maybe study at Harvard University, publish your work as far across the globe as Australia.

Yeah, you've heard of Josh Smith.

Note: "Receipts and Business Cards" was first published by *OCCULUM*, "The Last Scene of Struggling" was first published by *Ghost City Review*, and "Every You Every Me" was first published by *Hamilton Arts & Letters*.

The Last Scene of Struggling

I know where it is.
I know where the bottle is.
It's in a bag, taped under the lid of the toilet tank.

And you know what's in that bottle:
Jack Daniel's Tennessee Whiskey!

I quit drinking for the third time, last week.
My wife cleaned out the liquor cabinet,
the basement cooler, even the shoebox in the attic
that I didn't think she knew about.

But I snuck one by, because *I knew*.

I knew that THIS ASSHOLE was going to do 30mph
where it's 55, for fifteen fucking minutes!

I was mad when I realized it was a no-passing zone.
and livid five minutes later,
when he hadn't turned his blinker off.
When I got close enough to see the cell phone in his hands,
I was ready to kill.

YOU MISERABLE, ARROGANT SHITHEAD!

I'm not a bad guy. I get angry, but hey,
I don't beat my wife, or set the neighbor's cat on fire.

But if God himself doesn't drop an asteroid on this prick,
I swear to Jeebus, I'm gonna grab that bottle,
and I'm gonna pour myself a drink.

And then another. And then another.
Until the bottle is empty.
And then I'm gonna buy another. And another.
And some fucking pills too, Lord.
And I'm going to sit on my toilet, and I'm gonna drink,

I'm gonna swallow pills, and I'm gonna smoke.

Yeah, I almost forgot that!
I'm gonna drink, and smoke, and swallow pills
until I go out like Fat Elvis.

Because it's either him or me, God:
you can't have us both!
Either you drop an asteroid on this prick,
or me and Jack are checking out.

Tick, tock, Lord.
Tick, fucking tock.

Spare Sarcasm

As he lay there, a pile of grunge with feet,
a defeated voice croaked from his crust-covered lips,

'Scuse me sir, could you spare a little sarcasm
for a man down on his luck?

The few teeth that loved him enough
    to stay planted in his bleeding gums
    ran every direction but straight,
    shaping all of his sentences into questions.

I don't need a lot sir?
That sure is a nice suit?
Suit that nice, y'ought to have just a lil' sarcasm to spare?

Trapped by the traffic light,
    overpowered by his most odious odor,
    I addressed the man of mange and malaise.
With a cock of the head I roared,
Spare sarcasm? In this economy?!

Baby Oil Can Never Go Wrong

If you don't know how to pronounce someone's name,
don't struggle, strain, and sound it out.
It's better to butcher it with confidence—
you might even get it right.

If the speed limit is sixty,
you can expect traffic to drive eighty.
If you drive eighty in a sixty, you can expect construction.
No one cares if your puns were intended.
Stop calling everybody you don't like, a *hipster*.
You're just making hipsters ironically cooler.

Regardless of your opinion about these sentiments,
never forget: *baby oil can never go wrong.*

Some advice for aspiring artists:
Musicians–you're gonna fail.
Comedians–you're gonna fail.
Poets–you're gonna fail in iambic pentameter.
Painters–you're gonna fail.
Filmmakers–you're gonna fail expensively.
Nobody actually likes egg nog.

Young straight men:
fistfights only attract cops and lawyers;
if another man compliments you, be flattered.
If another man compliments your partner, be flattered.
Unless they put a hand where it doesn't belong,
it's all good.
Billy Joel—he's welcome on any playlist.

You may be exempt from a few of these edicts.
Some of these declarations may disquiet you.
But barring no one, you must epigraph in your heart,
no matter what you may have heard:
Baby oil can never go wrong.
Ever.

River Below

Nine-hundred dollars for three weeks,
sixth floor, right off the elevator and comes with a balcony.
It still has the lemon lotion smell of the Russian woman
    who slept here the night before—
two packets of her instant oatmeal on top of the fridge.

They're mine now:
the oatmeal, dollar store matchbooks,
green and silver plastic utensils.

This is my home away from everything I know.
No more steel mill shadows.
No more lakeshore sunsets.

Everything I knew is erased
    by the Red Line, Orange Line, *last stop Forest Hills,*
    timetables of trains and maps of a campus
    thumbtacked to a corkboard labeled *Goals.*

My scent erases hers in this borrowed bed,
my reflection in the window fills the river below.

I learn whether who I am is who I'm meant to be.

Ruminations I May Not Have Had, Had My Car Not Broken Down

Is it silence that makes the air cold,
or does the cold permit no sound?

I've never needed to know the name of this park until now.

Shrubbery grown wild smells like unwashed hair.

Sometimes it looks as if trees are only planted to
create clearings, openings, trails
from which wedding parties make their grand debut.

Spider webs showcase trophy kills;
if flies could scream, we would hear nothing else.

The furry creatures have more than they can appreciate,
but only in these limited acres.

Errant debris reminds us we exist;
this is not a mirage—as best as I can tell, anyway.

Costume for a Gutterball

With hair shaggy, clothes ratty
I'm begging *not* to be taken seriously.
I love to pretend I'm not capable.

Why kick down a door I could easier walk through,
fight for no prize,
give warning?

I will keep my eyelids half-open,
let shoulders droop and arms hang:
wear the costume for a gutterball.

But when these clothes are shed,
my hands raised,
eyes opened—

I will shock,
devour,
leave nothing left.

Receipts and Business Cards

The business cards are a roadmap across my coffee table,
the sweat-stained timeline of where I've gone and
neglected to go,
numbers I don't call back, and emails I'll never send.
I play games with these business cards.

B7
I could have done a radio interview.

N18
They wanted me to speak at a school.

G56
Bingo. There's that poem I started writing
somewhere between Orlando and Evansville.
The other half is on a receipt, for batteries
somewhere in Canada.

The receipts are a supplement; they provide
 topography for the map.

A bodega deep in the city:
I bought a bandana and a quart of iced tea.
8:57pm

230 miles between gas stations on the turnpike.
3:04 and 7:18pm

They sit on my coffee table in piles that slope and spill,
and threaten to ensnare.

They fall all over my clothing-patched floor when I sneeze
or gesture vigorously,
but they do not get put in their rightful place.
They are a warning:

Do not disturb. This man cannot answer you.
This man is held prisoner.
Go away.

Every You Every Me

Before the return flight was booked,
after the _______________ (weather event).

Before the ____________ (food/meal),
after the miscarriage.

Before the late-night arthouse flicks,
after the __________ (relative) Jamie waxing accident.

Before changing careers,
after __________ (alcohol) ___________ (body part).

Before 5am wake-up calls,
after we lost _______________ (pet name).

Before all-you-can-pick blueberries,
after _________________ (politician),

I have loved you.
Every me and every you.

Hey, How Long Does it Take to Pick Out a Pair of Shoes, What's Going On In There?

What about the middle times of just being with someone?
Hour after hour, day after day, for years on end… – *Dave Attell*

"Do you even care if we miss it?!"

We aren't going to be late,
if we just hit every green light,
find a parking spot without delay...
"If we leave right now, we can make up time!"

This. Always. Happens.
No respect for me, no respect for scheduling!
Every time, I have to smooth things over.
"If you can't pick, I'll pick for you!"

If we make it on time,
I'll go back to church.
I will donate to charity.
If we leave now,
"I'll get you ice cream on the way back!"

I might as well start getting undressed.
There's a TV dinner in the freezer,
or I might just go to sleep early.
"I'm taking my jacket off."

It's not like we have the senator's heart in a cooler.
We won't miss anything important.
Happy spouse, happy house.

"Hey, take as long as you need, Pookie.
As a matter of fact,
we'd spend half the money
if we just order food
and snuggle up in our footie pajamas.
Do you even care if we miss it?"

Gary Earl Ross

Gary Earl Ross is a retired University of Buffalo Professor and fiction writer, author of the AfroFuturism novel *Blackbird Rising*, and of *Wheel of Desire*, and *Shimerville*. His play, *Matter of Intent* was the recipient of the 2005 Edgar Award for Drama from the Mystery Writers of America. His plays include *Murder Squared, The Scavenger's Daughter, The Guns of Christmas, The Mark of Cain*, and The *Trial of Trayvon Martin*. Ross's first Buffalo-based Gideon Rimes mystery novel was published in 2017 by Black Opal Books, with sequel soon to be released.

For the Man Whose Son My Son Killed

You must understand this: my son
called me after his first firefight,
distraught that he had taken life
when I taught him to cherish it.
He called me, said he felt weird
and needed to talk to somebody.
Who better than the father who
carried him in a backpack, read
him a bedtime story each night,
and would always love him?
I'm here, I said. Tell me about it.
He did, and I listened, offering
mmm-hmms and yesses and words
of comfort when his voice caught.

Afterward he felt better and returned
to his duties in this dubious war.
Meanwhile, I was relieved he had
survived another day of the insanity.
On his second tour his vehicle hit a
roadside bomb. Bleeding from his
eyes because of a concussion, he flew
to the military hospital in Germany and
later came home. Again I was relieved.
Today, on the first leg of his third trip
to the Twilight Zone we've made of
your home, he called. I was glad to hear
his voice. Glad every damn time, ever
terrified your experience will be mine.

Later, when NPR broadcast a wailing
Iraqi father who'd lost two sons in this
chaos, I thought of you for the first time,
wondered if you were that father. It was

purely chance that your son aimed at mine
and mine squeezed off an auto burst first.
Two—no *three* fathers in agony because
our leaders are all fools. Still, someone
should recognize your pain. I do, sir,
and so does my son, himself a father.
We are both sorry for your loss.

The Disappearing Father Trick

all fathers disappear from the stage
some of them do so much too early
before children appreciate the magic
that daddy will—*poof!*—reappear at
the end of the day or week or month

too many fathers never reappear
the worst vanish by choice, forcing
children to see there is no magic
the best do so reluctantly, for the
world and its impossible hungers
are tricks beyond their control

but my dad always came back
from war, from work, from travel
now, for his final illusion, he disappears
slowly, memory by memory, synapse
by synapse, pound by pound, a wisp
dispersing into the stagnant air and
muted fluorescence of a nursing home

Explaining Gray Hair to My Children

When you look at me you see gray hair on my head,
morning salt on my cheeks,
white threads in my mustache,
an old man full of old ideas, but in the mirror I see
someone who once had a copperhead
slither over his foot;
who has fallen out of trees, off fences, off a roof,
out of favor; broken bones, his own
and those of a couple others,
broken hearts and often had his own heart broken
(bones, at least, can be counted and
heal so much faster);
who as a boy fought five at once and won
but as a man who'd studied karate
saw the wisdom of talk to avoid a barroom brawl;
who at 12 watched Jack Ruby shoot
Lee Harvey Oswald and is now friends with the
CBS cameraman who filmed the killing;
who himself twice stared down the barrel of a cocked,
    loaded gun, one held by a jittery cop, the other by a
    frightened, angry boy;
who walked away from a '68 Skylark
totaled by a tractor-trailer;
who's visited many countries and nearly every state in
    person, but seen infinite worlds and times and ideas
    in 4,000 plus books;
who worked in factories, stores, on a truck dock,
in a head shop with rolling papers, pipes,
with Janis and Jimi in blacklight;
who's marched and chanted and protested—
for this, against that;
who's painted houses and models, built bookcases,
written books; had dinner with Vincent Price,
drinks with Toni Morrison,

laughs with Melvin van Peebles,
interviews with Amy Goodman;
who's traveled great distances just to ride
a world class roller coaster or attend a classic
play or stand before an astonishing work of art,
and will always regret not having studied
a musical instrument;
who at 40, atop a mountain, saw an eagle
snatch lunch out of the sky,
and to celebrate turning 50
free fell 200 feet attached to a steel cable and
just because they were there
snorkeled in a cage amid 15 sharks;
who's turned his telescope on planets, nebulae,
and Galilean moons while teaching words
to remedy ignorance and injustice on earth;
who can say, "I love you" in ten tongues but
"I hate you" in just one;
who's made love—with your mothers,
and a select few others— in beds, trains, boats,
cars, beneath the sun, beneath the stars,
even with two unacquainted women who drank
with O.J. Simpson and once, like Sonny
Corleone, at somebody else's wedding.
So don't ignore all this steel as it fades to snow.
Every single strand has been earned and I wear
each one proudly.
I'm more than an old man
don't know nothin' 'bout nothin'.
I've lived and laughed and loved and lost and
 learned to live anew.
And I savor the telling of each and every tale.

Janna Willoughby- Lohr

Janna Willoughby-Lohr is a poet, spoken word artist, musician, and entrepreneur. As owner of *Papercraft Miracles*, a solar-powered company, she creates hand-crafted paper products such as wedding invitations, paper bouquets, albums, and stationery of all kinds using recycled and natural materials. Janna is an editor of the long-running women's poetry publication, *Earth's Daughters*. As a musician, Janna performs as activist rapper MC Vendetta, and with her band, *The Bloodthirsty Vegans*. Janna is mother to Vernon and Thurgood.

Black Thumbs

At 8:30 it all came,
the deals you made with wickedness.
The fear that I can't forget
rumbles to the surface.

The last straw has drunk up
every ounce of soul I've got
and your seed still isn't watered.

I thought that I could plant you,
pretend that I'm a gardener,
hoping that my deeds would thrive.

But how could I not see
that these thumbs are not
green, but black?

Or that black thumbs
always push *too* hard
or not hard enough?

Something happens.
The seed doesn't make it.

I must think of this
as a burial
in hopes for tulips
the next time around.

When the tips come up,
spreading the earth
like virgin legs

and entering this world,
I will feel the delight
of being warmed under
some other sun,
until again
getting burned
in some other life.

Claw-foot

When I was growing up
we didn't have a shower,
only this beast of a tub.

Sometimes I was convinced
that they'd built
the apartment around it,
no way to fit it through the doors.

That big old claw-foot tub,
raw-rubbed enamel
flaky-painted belly
gotta turn em' off tight duckbill faucets,
the stain from the drip—the times I forgot,

the tub is still a glory;
the prize feature in a not-so-classy world

Mama did the best
with all the class
she could afford:

the lip of the tub
lined with rows of soaps

and washes, five different
kinds of conditioner,
the water-stained bright blue pitcher
tucked into the just-right nook
between the wall and the tub
and the toilet tank.

Hooked onto the side of the tub,
near the pitcher,
brass soap dish, not getting any younger,
with the open round sponge basket on top -
never held a sponge as long as I remember -
sitting right in between the rungs
was a small, lead-colored cup
always brimming full of too many cigarette butts.
I can still smell them
if I picture her there.

Dance Partner

The way you become light on top of me—
balancing closely as a dance partner should,
fills my roses with heat
then coats them with dew.

Your tango takes hold of my hand,
and how I love when
you twirl around my hips like
lions stalking their lovers in the wild.

Then your samba slides something
sumptuous along silken sunsets,
your love slipping its hands
into my night sky.

Fox trot fox you're hot to trot,
varying your speed like a driver,
pulling into the lead, grinning,
you whirling sexy dervish of a man.

Flamenco heat pulls the sweat from my face,
your breath and my taste locked in rhythms,
glances, lips held so close,
like questions waiting for answers.

Last dance of the evening,
you can't wait to pull me tight,
with our breath growing quickly
we both come into the night.

The Bright One

The moon is bright enough
to light any path.

But still I keep this flame
flickering on the back porch
and the sensible winds come
and try to put this fire out.

As soon as the wind dies down,
I rekindle this fire and it burns brightly
and far too hot to really know you,
just how my face appeared in your glow.

Maybe you are just the bright one,
Like a lantern in the woods,
I can only see a few feet around you,
the rest of the world seems black.

My heart cannot adjust to the light
with the dancing uncertainty of your flicker—
a light that I don't need if the moon is this bright.

I have to lick my fingers
and pinch this wick,

hear the spit sizzle,
feel it burn away.

Sara Ries

Sara Ries, a Buffalo native, holds an MFA in poetry from Chatham University. Her first book, *Come In, We're Open*, won the Stevens Poetry Manuscript Competition and was published in June 2010 by the *NFSPS Press*. Her poem, "Fish Fry Daughter," was selected by Ted Kooser for his *American Life in Poetry* column. She and her husband, Thaddeus, moved to St. Petersburg, FL in February 2018 after teaching EFL in four diverse regions of Colombia. Her chapbook, *Snow Angels on the Living Room Floor*, was released in December 2018 by *Finishing Line Press*.

I Pour More Steaming Rivers

We need to talk, Joanne says
Friday night at The Plaka
as I scoop up tartar sauce
and drop the globs
into one ounce soufflé cups.

It's my fourth job in three months
since I said *Dad, I love our little red diner,*
but I've been here all my life—

It was 12:15, what used to be lunch rush.
He was scrubbing platters as I sorted silverware.
I never thought my life would end up like this, he said,
and I remembered what he once told me, that his dream
before the diner was to pack up the van and drive
until a city felt like home.

Joanne's earrings dangle like running dogs
yanked when the chain goes straight.
Her eyes are pots of strong coffee
that sat too long on the burner.
My request-off days are folded between her fingers.
I don't want to compete with poetry, she says.

I wish I could say that I told Joanne *It's no competition,*
releasing myself from this apron, and into the silk river sky
where stars are lights for people to float on,

but I picture myself wrinkled & grey,
slipping on tartar sauce. A carafe shatters
on the counter's edge, each shard a year of my life.
I get up, straighten my smock, go around with coffee.
But I no longer laugh at: *My eyes are turning brown or*

I'll float away. I wear their banter like varicose veins.

Sorry I tell Joanne, then pour more steaming rivers
into thick sturdy mugs, anchors for lonely hands.
Coffee? I say and the old man answers
One more cup will hoist my sails, a line I've never heard
so I grab my pen and write it down
like it's the only poem left.

Teenage Waitress

I was still getting used to my hips,
which developed wide so they'd ram
into curves of counters as I'd swing around corners
with coffee & creamers in my parents' diner.

Two men at a back booth eyed me
up and down. The scruffy beard one asked
Can I get anything on the menu?
I said yes. He asked if *I* was on the menu.
I laughed. They sat with one knee facing,
claiming me like an arrow.

The other man pointed to their rusted work van
parked behind my father's pickup,
said he had handcuffs and whipped cream in there,
that he'd get them if I wanted.

They wore slimy smirks
and mouths hung open.
(I wore a t-shirt and jeans,
if you must know.)

I laughed, not knowing what else to utter.
I could taste the filth that covered them.

The words I should have said were wedged
like crumbs in the booth cracks. It was the day
I learned to wither, become smaller,
so there was less of me for the taking.

I told my dad. He was cooking faster
than a shoeshiner with a line of hanging
guest checks. He huffed, shook his head.
He did not have time for this. I couldn't tell
if he was mad at me or them.

These are the stories that stay with us
like infections that won't heal;
gum stuck under the countertop
which goes with the counter to the landfill.

I served the men their sandwiches.
I could feel them staring at my ass as I walked away,
and my body blamed itself.

They left and never came back,
but it wasn't my father who told them not to.
He went by the saying:
The customer's always right.

My father never kicked anyone out of our diner,
not these guys, nor Don, who I'm sure is dead by now.
Once when I was eating chocolate chip pancakes,
he towered over me and said,
Watch your shape and *fat is ugly* and
You're beginning to look more and more
like your mother.

But that is another poem, and another kind
of shrinking.

Cigarettes, Meat Fat & Ice Cream

I.

Every Saturday, Uncle John rang our doorbell
and from my room I listened
for galloping feet and the click of the lock.

He never ate dinner at our table,
no matter how many times I pulled up a chair.
He'd say *I'm fine right here*, and stand by our shoes,
plate on the back counter. His greasy hair
was combed, teeth crooked, chipped.
As I cleared our plates, he'd say
The fat is the best part, and he gathered our scraps,
except for the pieces I hid in my napkin.

He also loved ice cream
always asked for more
even when Brian and I piled it on,
laughing hysterically, sure he'd never finish it.

Want to sit on the patio, shoot the breeze?
he'd ask whoever was closest. Sometimes we did
on furniture he built with Dad. *I have a best friend,*
he said, as he puffed a cigarette. *Who?*
He lifted his chin and smiled *Your father.*
He pressed the embers to the ashtray, pulled another
from his stretched shirt pocket. Once,
when my parents were away, he lit one for me
and I told him my secrets.

At dusk, he'd give us bear hugs
trapping my nose against his flannel
which reeked of stale sweat and Marlboros
as Dad rummaged through the fridge,
packed a bag with leftovers

to get him through the week.

II.

November, a week before I would turn sixteen,
the grass wore a thin white veil; I couldn't stop shivering.
I could hear Uncle John: *Eat something.*
He said this whenever I was cold.

When the doorbell didn't ring,
I sat by the window and waited
for his small black car
to sputter up the driveway,
dinner hardening under pot lids.

We searched for his trail:
pennies against the red house bricks,
a higher pile of cigarette butts.
Sometimes, if no one was home,
he left us little hellos.

Sunday evening, Dad took me
to Uncle John's grey apartment
while Mom and Brian waited.
I followed Dad up three flights of stairs.
He knocked, then rammed the door down
and we went in, the air bloated
with final breaths

and found him. He was lying in bed
in jeans and flannel and boots
on top of smoothed-out blankets.

III.

Dad sobbed as he drove us home;
the car swerved. He pounded his fists against
the steering wheel, cried *My brother, my brother—*

and then, the clouds parted
and a river of light poured through.
There's Uncle John, Dad said
and all I could answer was *Yes*.

Joe Todaro

Joe Todaro was born and raised in the North Park area of Buffalo, migrated in the early 90s to the West Side Elmwood environs during a time of Sunday Rose Garden drum circles, clinic defense, Circular Word Books, Topic Cafe, 3B's, Cybele's and the original Pink Flamingo; conspiracies hatched over nocturnal omelets, drying out at Towne Restaurant and breakfasts at Preservation Hall: of alternative currency, of Network of Light, Good River, Urban Epiphany, Classics on Elmwood recitals and a legendary Diamond Tribe song sojourn now known as Cheaper Than Vinyl.

Joe had a big return in 2002 from the Bay Area after a four year existential ruse; then as now, and here in current form.

Sunrise

Red mug - coffee,
    knees up reclining,
    the feeling between my eyebrows when I can
        concentrate,
        telling me I am present;
here
    focused:
        the glide of this pen,
        pores of this page beading
        with ink,
    when the clench in my chest is just a curio
        as with this mind's din-flood of tangents
        - celebrated;
various sound-sources about my sphere,
and that recognition:
    downstairs front door locks,
        thuds on front steps,

car motor starts
         behind a window at my back - my window,
    light hovers from kitchen, living room lamp,
         computer,
         daylight through clouds;
I can like these and this
    that contains them;
    thus - reminded of myself -
    I am.

Zen Dough

The student asked his master,
        "What is the sound of one hand clapping?"
        to which the master swiftly slapped him
        full-force on his left cheek,

and the student, in reflex,
        using his full weight, drove his fist
        into his master's abdomen;
        doubled over and falling

to the floor, the master
        pronounced him
        enlightened.

Soliloquy

Softly, today,
the sudden trail snapping

around you: see it as it slips,
and the god you knew;

those things that persevered,
their tracks across your limbs,

you, certainty, pulled
from these wrists, covering

the gravel.

www.ingramcontent.com/pod-product-compliance
Lightning Source LLC
Chambersburg PA
CBHW060932140726
47996CB00001B/473